Revealing Antiquity

· 8 ·

G. W. Bowersock, General Editor

HYPATIA OF ALEXANDRIA

MARIA DZIELSKA

Translated by F. Lyra

Harvard University Press
Cambridge, Massachusetts
London, England

Adapted and translated from the unpublished manuscript.

First Harvard University Press paperback edition, 1996

Library of Congress Cataloging-in-Publication Data

Dzielska, Maria.
[Hypatia z Aleksandrii. English]
Hypatia of Alexandria / Maria Dzielska ; translated by F. Lyra.
p.   cm. — (Revealing antiquity ; 8)
Includes bibliographical references and index.
ISBN 0-674-43775-6 (alk. paper) (cloth)
ISBN 0-674-43776-4 (pbk.)
1. Hypatia, d. 415.   2. Women philosophers—Egypt.
3. Alexandrian school.   I. Title.   II. Series.
B667.H84D95   1995
186'.4—dc20
[B]
94-24499
CIP

Piis manibus Miroslai

ACKNOWLEDGMENTS

The idea of a book on Hypatia occurred to me as I was doing research on the life and work of Synesius of Cyrene. When reading his letters filled with admiration for Hypatia's soul and mind, I felt a need to learn more about this extraordinary Alexandrian woman, scholar, and philosopher whose life and spiritual individuality have sustained interest in her for many centuries.

While working on the book I received help and encouragement from various people and institutions. I began research on Hypatia in 1988 at the Ashmolean Library during a short scholarly visit at Oxford. A fellowship from the Trustees of Harvard University in 1990 gave me the opportunity to resume research at the Center for Byzantine Studies at Dumbarton Oaks in Washington, D.C. The book would have never materialized without the scholarly support of the Center, with its magnificent library, the courtesy of its staff, and especially the advice and guidance of Professor Angeliki E. Laiou, Director of the Center.

I am particularly grateful to G. W. Bowersock, whose long-term support and consistent intellectual inspiration sustained me through moments of doubt and helped bring the project to fruition. I wish to express profound gratitude to my fellowship colleague at Dumbarton Oaks, Stephen Gero of the Orientalisches Seminar of the University of Tübingen, for his invaluable bibliographical assistance; without his constant mindfulness of and interest in the progress of my research, I would have missed the latest publications on Hypatia and her era. While writing the book, I have relied upon Alan Cameron's appreciative understanding of my scholarly problems. Ever generous with advice, he obliged me with the manuscript of his book *Barbarians and Politics at the Court of Arcadius* and copies of his articles. I have encountered equally warm support from Ihor Ševčenko, Ewa Wipszycka (Warsaw University), and Maciej Salamon (Jagiellonian University, Kraków). To all of them, and to F. Lyra for his translation, I extend sincere gratitude.

CONTENTS

HYPATIA OF ALEXANDRIA

・|・

THE LITERARY
LEGEND
OF HYPATIA

The Modern Tradition

Long before the first scholarly attempts to reconstruct an accurate image of Hypatia, her life—marked by the dramatic circumstances of her death—had been imbued with legend. Artistically embellished, distorted by emotions and ideological biases, the legend has enjoyed wide popularity for centuries, obstructing scholarly endeavors to present Hypatia's life impartially, and it persists to this day. Ask who Hypatia was, and you will probably be told: "She was that beautiful young pagan philosopher who was torn to pieces by monks (or, more generally, by Christians) in Alexandria in 415." This pat answer would be based not on ancient sources, but on a mass of belletristic and historical literature, a representative sample of which is surveyed in this chapter. Most of these works present Hypatia as an innocent victim of the fanaticism of nascent Christianity, and her murder as marking the banishment of freedom of inquiry along with the Greek gods.

Hypatia first appeared in European literature in the eighteenth century. In the era of skepticism known historically as the Enlightenment, several writers used her as an instrument in religious and philosophical polemic.

In 1720 John Toland, in youth a zealous Protestant, published a long historical essay titled *Hypatia or, the History of a Most Beautiful, Most Virtuous, Most Learned and in Every Way Accomplished Lady; Who Was Torn to Pieces by the Clergy of Alexandria, to Gratify the Pride, Emulation, and Cruelty of the Archbishop, Commonly but Undeservedly Titled St. Cyril*. Though basing his account of Hypatia on sources such as the tenth-century encyclopedia *Suda,* Toland begins by asserting that the male part of humanity has been forever disgraced by the murder of "the incarnation of beauty and wisdom"; men must always "be ashamed, that any could be found among them of so brutal and savage a disposition, as, far from being struck with admiration at so much beauty, innocence, and knowledge, to stain their barbarous hands with her blood, and their impious souls with the indelible character of sacrilegious murderers." In unfolding the story of Hypatia's life and death, Toland focuses on the Alexandrian clergy, headed by the patriarch Cyril: "A Bishop, a Patriarch, nay a Saint, was the contriver of so horrid a deed, and his clergy the executioners of his implacable fury."[1]

The essay produced a stir in ecclesiastical circles and was speedily answered by Thomas Lewis in a pamphlet, *The History of Hypatia, a Most Impudent School-Mistress of Alexandria. In Defense of Saint Cyril and the Alexandrian Clergy from the Aspersions of Mr. Toland*.[2] But for the most part Toland's work enjoyed a favorable reception among the Enlightenment elite. Voltaire exploited the figure of Hypatia to express his repugnance for the church and revealed religion. In a style not unlike Toland's, he writes about Saint Cyril and the Alexandrian clergy in *Examen important de Milord Bolingbroke ou le tombeau du fanatisme* (1736). Hypatia's death was "a bestial murder perpetrated by Cyril's tonsured hounds, with a fanatical gang at their heels."[3] She was murdered, Voltaire asserts, because she believed in the Hellenic gods, the laws of rational Nature, and the capacities of the human mind free of imposed dogmas. Thus did religious fanaticism lead to the martyrdom of geniuses and to the enslavement of the spirit.

Voltaire returns to Hypatia in his *Dictionnaire philosophique*. There he asserts that she "taught Homer and Plato in Alexandria during the reign of Theodosius II" and that the events leading to her death were instigated by Saint Cyril, who "loosed the Christian rabble on her." Though not neglecting to divulge his sources—Damascius, *Suda,* and "the most learned men of the age"—Voltaire makes quite cavalier use of them; and in the midst of serious accusations against Cyril and the Christians, he offers a coarse, asinine salon witticism about his favorite heroine: "When one strips beautiful women naked, it is not to massacre them." In truth, we are left in the dark as to whether the "sage of Ferney" is deriding his readers, the ideas that he is promulgating with such enthusiasm, or Hypatia. Voltaire expresses hope that the patriarch Cyril asked God for forgiveness and that God indeed had mercy on him; Voltaire himself prays for the patriarch: "I beseech the merciful father to have pity on his soul."[4]

Toland's and Voltaire's reductive accounts of Hypatia mark the genesis of a legend that mixes truth and falsehood. Had they consulted their ancient sources with greater perception, they would have detected in them a far more complex personality. This "victim of superstition and ignorance" not only believed in the redemptive powers of reason but also sought god through religious revelation. Above all, she was stubborn and intensely moral, no less a proponent of asceticism than the dogmatic Christians whom Voltaire and others depicted as ruthless enemies of "truth and progress."

Influenced by Enlightenment ideas, neo-Hellenism, and Voltaire's literary and philosophical style, Edward Gibbon elaborated the legend of Hypatia. In *The Decline and Fall of the Roman Empire* he identifies Cyril as the perpetrator of all conflicts in Alexandria at the beginning of the fifth century, including the murder of Hypatia.[5] According to Gibbon, Hypatia "professed the religion of the Greeks" and taught publicly in both Athens and Alexandria. I do not know the source of Gibbon's first claim; the latter reflects an erroneous interpretation of Damascius' account in *Suda*. Like Toland and Voltaire,

Gibbon retails Damascius' story about Cyril's burning envy of Hypatia, who was "in the bloom of beauty, and in the maturity of wisdom," surrounded by disciples and persons "most illustrious for their rank or merit" and always "impatient to visit the female philosopher." Hypatia was murdered by "a troop of savage and merciless fanatics" instigated by Cyril, and the crime was never punished, apparently because "superstition [Christianity] perhaps would more gently expiate the blood of a virgin, than the banishment of a saint." This representation of "the Alexandrian crime" perfectly fitted Gibbon's theory that the rise of Christianity was the crucial cause of the fall of the ancient civilization. He used the circumstances of Hypatia's life to document this thesis and to show the difference between the old world and the new: reason and spiritual culture (Hypatia) versus dogmatism and barbaric absence of restraint (Cyril and Christianity).[6]

The figure of Hypatia appears briefly and allusively in many other eighteenth-century works, including Henry Fielding's droll satiric novel *A Journey from This World to the Next* (1743). Describing Hypatia as "a young lady of greatest beauty and merit," Fielding states that "those dogs, the Christians, murdered her."[7]

But it was in the mid-nineteenth century that the literary legend of Hypatia reached its apex. Charles Leconte de Lisle published two versions of a poem titled *Hypatie,* one in 1847 and another in 1874.[8] In the first version Hypatia is a victim of the laws of history and not of a Christian "plot," as Voltaire contended.[9] Leconte de Lisle views the circumstances of Hypatia's death with historical detachment, from the perspective that history cannot be identified with a single culture or system of belief. The era of Hypatia simply faded away, replaced by a new one with its own rules and forms. As a believer in the old deities and a lover of reason and sensual beauty, she became a symbolic victim of the changing circumstances of history. "Mankind, in its headlong course, struck you and cursed you."[10]

In the second version of the poem Leconte de Lisle reverts to an anti-Christian interpretation of Hypatia's death. It is Christians who are guilty of the crime, not "historical necessity":

> The vile Galilean struck you and cursed you;
> But in falling, you became even greater! And now, alas!
> The spirit of Plato and the body of Aphrodite
> Have withdrawn forever to the fair skies of Hellas!

This version echoes Toland's anticlerical, and specifically anti-Catholic, motif.[11] As the legend develops, that motif is reinforced.

Both of Leconte de Lisle's Hypatia poems manifest confidence in the permanence of the essential values of antiquity. As one of the founders of the Parnassian school of poetry, which drew inspiration from classical antiquity, Leconte de Lisle loved classical literature. He not only translated Greek poets and dramatists; he regarded Hellenism as the fulfillment of the ideals of humanity, beauty combined with wisdom. Thus for Leconte de Lisle, despite her death Hypatia lives on in the Western imagination as the embodiment of physical beauty and the immortality of the spirit, just as the pagan ideals of Greece have molded Europe's spirituality.

> She alone survives, immutable, eternal;
> Death can scatter the trembling universes
> But Beauty still dazzles with her fire,
>   and all is reborn in her,
> And the worlds are still prostrate beneath her white feet!

Leconte de Lisle's admiration for the Greeks' excellence and Hellenic ideas about the supernatural world is also expressed in a short dramatic work, "Hypatie et Cyrille" (1857).[12] In it we find the same Romantic longing for ancient Greece, where people lived in harmony with the beauty of divine nature and in conformity with the teachings of their philosophers—the same longing that resonates in Hölderlin's poems, the classics of "Weimar humanism," and the works of the English neo-

Hellenists. Here Leconte de Lisle attempts to reconcile pagan philosophy with Christianity.

Plato's beautiful and wise disciple tries to convince the stern patriarch Cyril that there is only a small difference between Neoplatonism and Christianity: "The words are slightly different, the sense is very much the same." Hypatia admits that the person of Christ is holy to her, but she also feels affinity with the gods enrobed in the eternal fabrics of the cosmos. The deities reveal themselves in the beauty of nature, in the intelligence of the astral bodies, in the wonder of art, in the spirituality of sages searching for truth. Cyril's pronouncement, "Your gods are reduced to dust, at the feet of the victorious Christ," elicits Hypatia's passionate credo:

> You're mistaken, Cyril. They live in my heart.
> Not as you see them—clad in transient forms,
> Subject to human passions even in heaven,
> Worshiped by the rabble and worthy of scorn—
> But as sublime minds have seen them
> In the starry expanse that has no dwellings:
> Forces of the universe, interior virtues,
> Harmonious union of earth and heaven
> That delights the mind and the ear and the eye,
> That offers an attainable ideal to all wise men
> And a visible splendor to the beauty of the soul.
> Such are my Gods!

"Hypatie et Cyrille," full of exaltation and Romantic rapture over the Greeks' "heaven," ends with a description of the bishop's anger. He has no understanding of Hypatia's belief in the world of divine intelligences and the natural beauty of the universe. Cyril threatens her and her world with the curse of oblivion, extinction of the ancient culture.

Leconte de Lisle's poems were known and widely read in the nineteenth century; and the image of Hypatia in love with the ideal forms of the visible world—in contrast to the closed spheres of Cyril's rigidly dogmatic Christianity—has survived to our time. Even today we tend to associate the figure of Hypatia with de Lisle's line, "Le souffle de Platon et le corps d'Aphrodite," the spirit of Plato and the body of Aphrodite.

Leconte de Lisle's younger contemporary Gérard de Nerval referred to Hypatia in an 1854 work,[13] and in 1888 Maurice Barrès published a short story about Hypatia, "La vierge assassinée," in a collection titled *Sous l'oeil des barbares*. Barrès states in his preface that he wrote the story at the request of Leconte de Lisle, his "Parnassian master."[14] "La vierge assassinée" combines bucolic elements with a cool and austere presentation of philosophy and moral virtues.

The story opens as young Lucius meets the charming and beautiful Alexandrian courtesan Amaryllis on the banks of the Nile canal overgrown with water lilies. The marble of a temple and Greek sculptures glimmers beyond the trees, and we also see town buildings and ships anchored in the port. However, rich and beautiful Alexandria is in decline: "The town extends its arms over the ocean and seems to call the entire universe to its perfumed and feverish bed, to lend assistance during the death throes of a world and the formation of the ages to come."[15]

Walking to the Serapeum, where Hypatia (who is called Athénée in this story) is usually to be found, Lucius and Amaryllis encounter a crowd of Christians who are chasing Jews out of the city. The audience awaiting Athénée/Hypatia in the library of the Serapeum talk with alarm about "the Christian sect, which says it owes its convictions to the fact that the lenient temples have fallen into disrepute and age-old traditions have been abandoned." They recall that the Emperor Julian perished at the hands of a Christian while fighting to defend holy monuments of the past. One member of the audience attempts to induce the "Hellenes" to defend themselves against the "barbarians" using their methods, that is, cruelty and violence; otherwise "those barbarians will destroy you."

In the meantime a crowd of Christians begins to assail the Serapeum, calling for the death of Athénée, the symbol of paganism in the city. The mob forces its way into the interior of the shrine, where Athénée delivers a speech in praise of the Hellenic past and takes an oath of fidelity to the monuments of the past now being destroyed. Impressed by her speech, the mob desists, but its most zealous members continue to incite action. Athénée calmly awaits death. Lucius, Amaryllis, and their friends attempt to lead her out of the temple, but she refuses to abandon "the library and the statues of our forebears." Covering her face with a long veil, she gives herself up to the mob, which tears her to pieces. The Roman legions, which have just entered the city, are unable to rescue her. In the evening Amaryllis and Lucius find the divine remains "of the virgin of Serapis." Barrès assures us that the martyrdom of "the last of the Hellenes" will become the source of her apotheosis and enduring legend.

While Leconte de Lisle, Barrès, and others were writing about Hypatia in France, the English clergyman, novelist, and historian Charles Kingsley elaborated her legend in a long book titled *Hypatia or the New Foes with an Old Face* (1853).[16] Though originally intended as a historical study based on the author's research on Greek culture of the late empire and the history of Alexandria, it in fact took the form of a mid-Victorian romance with a strong anti-Catholic flavor. Kingsley detested priests and monks, with their vows of celibacy and their seclusion from the affairs of this world. In the book Cyril and the clergy around him exemplify the Catholic hierarchy and the segment of the Anglican clergy that opposed Kingsley; good Christians could find their virtues represented in the young monk, the converted Jew, the courtesan Pelagia, and Hypatia herself.

The action of the novel occurs chiefly in Alexandria. This large port city of the East, wealthy and poor, enlightened and primitive, with a heterogeneous population of Greeks, Egyptians, Jews, and—as Kingsley would have it—Goths, provides an appropriate medley of nationalities, trades, beliefs, and social classes, out of which emerge the central characters of the novel: the pagan philosopher Hypatia, the dogmatic and despotic patriarch Cyril, the ambitious and power-hungry prefect of Egypt Orestes, and the monk Philammon.

Hypatia incarnates "the spirit of Plato and the body of Aphrodite." Though barely twenty-five years old, she gives lectures in the Museion on Platonic and Neoplatonic philosophy. Throngs of young people surround her; she knows all the important people in the city and is herself a very influential person. Hypatia writes commentaries on Plotinus' works and, with her father Theon, studies the writings of ancient masters in mathematics and geometry. Her pagan erudition is an irritant to Christian circles in Alexandria. The patriarch Cyril sees to it that young Christians do not attend her lectures; he does not want them exposed, under her tantalizing influence, to Greek science and philosophy. When the young monk Philammon expresses a desire to attend, Cyril describes Hypatia to him as "subtler than the serpent, skilled in all the tricks of logic" and warns, "you will become a laughing-stock, and run away in shame."

Beautiful, wise, and virtuous, Hypatia displays some surprising features: a fierce hatred of Christianity and a Voltairean obdurateness rather than Neoplatonic benignity. She is full of contempt for the monks and the clergy, supercilious toward the creed that is alien to her civilization. She characterizes monks as "bigots, wild beasts of the desert, and fanatic intriguers, who in the words of Him they call their master, compass heaven and earth to make him twofold more the child of hell than themselves."

The monk Philammon is one of those whom Hypatia despises. He has been brought up in the desert and is completely under the spiritual influence of the patriarch. Prompted by curiosity and interest in Hypatia's fame, he attends one of her lectures with a view to condemning her teachings and converting her. Instead, he becomes one of her most devoted and loyal disciples. He discovers in Hypatia a deep religiosity that transcends simple belief in the Homeric deities, and their friendship, mixed with erotic overtones, lasts until Hypatia's death.

Kingsley presents the prefect Orestes as a cunning schemer, drunken and dissolute, with far-reaching political ambitions. Hoping to become emperor of Egypt and Africa and, perhaps later, the East, he supports the revolt of Heraclian, governor of West Africa. He draws Hypatia into these plans by proposing marriage to her. He arranges sumptuous gladiatorial games, dance performances, and other public revelries, promising Hypatia that they portend a renaissance of paganism. He assures her that these manifestations of a simple religiosity are only a transitory phase meant to win people's hearts; they will be soon replaced by a religiosity of a higher order.

Heraclian, in whom Orestes vests all his hopes, suffers defeat at the gates of Rome. Only then does Hypatia realize that she has been a victim of Orestes' deceptions and machinations. Her honesty, nobility, and faith in the sublime ideals of a resurrected Hellenic religiosity have been betrayed.

Kingsley's story of the conflict between Orestes and Cyril follows the account by the fifth-century church historian Socrates Scholasticus. A series of incidents bring escalating tensions between the prefect's people and the church. During street actions provoked by the monks the prefect himself sustains an injury. A rumor is spread that Hypatia is the cause of the unrest in the city, the sower of discord. And although at the last she is converted and baptized into Christianity, she is murdered by monks, the parabolans or church servants, and a Christian mob under the leadership of Peter the Reader. The murder provides an outlet for fanaticism, ignorance, and hidden lusts—Kingsley strongly emphasizes the erotic aspect of the act committed on the beautiful young woman.

Before her death Hypatia, deceived and disappointed by Orestes' lies, undergoes a spiritual crisis. Her conversion is effected through the beneficent influence of a former disciple, the Jew Raphael Aben-Ezra. After Hypatia's death he demands that Cyril identify the perpetrators. When the bishop refuses, Raphael warns Cyril that the kingdom of God he is erecting may turn out to be the kingdom of Satan, to which the patriarch may be condemned.

The memory of the crime against Hypatia lives on in Alexandria. Science and philosophy wither away, and with them the intellectual life of Alexandria. "Twenty years after Hypatia's death, philosophy was flickering down to the very socket. Hypatia's murder was its death-blow." The nascent Christian church in Egypt suffers disgrace and loses itself in trivial sectarian disputes and quarrels among clerics.

Kingsley's book was translated into several European languages, and several German historians even wrote dissertations on it.[17] His broad novelistic vision of "the last of the Hellenes" entertained readers around the world. His figure of Hypatia functions as a symbol of passing civilization, as the last victim of the struggle for the rescue of the perfect Grecian world of harmony, art and metaphysics, divinity and materialism, soul and body. Far more than the accounts of Toland, Voltaire, Barrès, or Leconte de Lisle, Kingsley's book promoted and sustained the notion that with the death of the last idealist of Hellenism, Greek values disappeared.

In the second half of the nineteenth century American and British positivists presented Hypatia as primarily a scientist, the last scholar in the Greek East. Thus the American scientist J. W. Draper, described as a "valiant defender of science against religion," considered Hypatia a heroic figure in the contest between two powers in European history: the free mind searching for truth in the material world versus superstitious religion (represented by the church) enslaving reason. This perspective renders the history of European thought very simple: from the death of Hypatia until the age of the Enlightenment Europe was draped in darkness; the Enlightenment (with its revolt against the authority of the church, revelation, and dogmas) conquered the darkness and reopened the clear sky of knowledge. The death of Hypatia was "one of those moments in which great general principles embody themselves in individuals. It is Greek philosophy under the appropriate form of Hypatia; ecclesiastical ambition under that of Cyril." After a graphic description of Hypatia's horrible death, Draper adds: "Though in his privacy St. Cyril and his friends might laugh at the end of his antagonist, his memory must bear the weight of the righteous indignation of posterity." He concludes: "Thus in the year 414 of our era, the position of philosophy in the intellectual metropolis of the world was determined; henceforth science must sink into obscurity and subordination. Its public existence will no longer be tolerated."[18]

Bertrand Russell, expressing similar sentiments, opens his history of Western European thought with a characterization of Saint Cyril: "His chief claim to fame is the lynching of Hypatia, a distinguished lady who, in an age of bigotry, adhered to the Neoplatonic philosophy and devoted her talents to mathematics . . . After this Alexandria was no longer troubled by philosophers."[19]

Hypatia became a figure in modern Italian literature as early as 1827, when Contessa Diodata Roero di Saluzzo published a two-volume poem, *Ipazia ovvero delle Filosofie*.[20] This work ventures beyond the legend into a fanciful biography of Hypatia that connects Hypatia with Christianity. This is a venerable tradition: elements of Hypatia's life were inscribed in the legend of Saint Catherine of Alexandria, for example.[21] Saluzzo portrays Hypatia as a disciple of Plotinus living with him in the "Alexandrian Lyceum" and unhappily in love with the Egyptian prince Isidore who fights for independence from Rome. Hypatia parts company with Isidore and, having been converted by Bishop Cyril, links her fate with that of the Christians. She dies in a church, at the foot of the Cross, killed with three blows of a sword by a treacherous priest.

Other Italian works present Hypatia in the context of the struggle between expiring paganism and an ascendant Christianity that destroys old values and imposes its own truths. In the chapter "Ipazia e le ultime lotte pagane" in his book on great men in history, Carlo Pascal reiterates the theme that connects Hypatia's death with the decline of philosophy and Mediterranean civilization in general.[22] Pascal, however, also introduces a new element into the literary tradition of Hypatia, one that resonates in our time: Hypatia's death is seen as an antifeminist act.

"Obviously the persecution against Hypatia stemmed to a great extent from this insolent and superstitious antifemale tendency." It brought about a profound change in the treatment of women. Formerly free, intellectually independent, and creative, they were suppressed into silence.

In 1978 two thematically related dramas by Mario Luzi were published in one volume: *Libro di Ipazia* and *Il messagero,* the latter about Synesius of Cyrene. *Libro di Ipazia* is not only a historical work, as G. Pampaloni remarks in his introduction;[23] it is also a drama of historicism. The story of Hypatia is meant to serve as testimony to the irreversibility of historical phases: the decline of Greek culture and the victory of the new order were inevitable. The drama begins in Alexandria, then moves to Cyrene, where Bishop Synesius fights the barbarians who are both threat and heralds of the destination of history.

A lament for the political and social decay of Alexandria opens the play. Its greatness is gone, and there are almost no traces of those "perennial flowerings" that made her famous. Orestes, the prefect of Egypt, complains to George, a well-known and respected Alexandrian, about the weakness and impotence of Alexandria's civil government. Insoluble problems confront them as a result of the forceful presence of pagans and fanaticism of the Christian masses. Orestes says that the city's Hellenes, the disciples of Proclus and Plotinus, "pour oil on water." But the daughter of Theon is kindling hostility and passions; as the gentle and wise woman philosopher turns into a formidable adversary, "her sweetness becomes horrible." Orestes is afraid of Cyril and incapable of restricting Hypatia's freedom of speech and that of her friends. So he asks George to join the ranks of the pagan intellectuals and to do everything in his power to stop them from publicly teaching Greek philosophy and religion.

The second act takes place in Synesius' house. Jone, a woman who lives with Synesius, and George beg Synesius to act in the cause of peace and order in the city and quell the storm that has been brewed by "the enchantress Hypatia." Synesius interprets the disturbances as a manifestation of the law of history: the Greek mind must be reconciled with the Christian logos; the highest reason calls for harmony between these two worlds.

In the third act Hypatia conducts a dialogue with herself. Her inner voice tells her that her time has come: "prepare yourself. Your hour is approaching." Weeping, Hypatia prepares for death: "Let me cry a little while longer and then I will come to wherever you may call me." At this moment Synesius enters; he begs her to stop propagating pagan philosophy and religion, for the entire city is in an uproar and in danger of a disaster. He tells her that the prefect has lost control over the situation; in addition, the prefect has quarreled with the bishop. Hypatia, however, stands by her truths and conduct. Synesius leaves Hypatia's house with the premonition that he will never see her again, but he is afraid of saying good-bye. He only blurts out, "Until tomorrow."

In the fourth and final act Synesius tells George about his failed mission. As he reiterates his opinion of Hypatia, Jone bursts in with the news of the murder and, at Synesius' behest, relates the circumstances in detail:

> "Well, she was speaking in the square to many people,
> speaking about the present God and they were listening to
>   her in silence,
> in a stupor, both followers and adversaries.
> But a fanatic horde interrupted,
> hands and hands came down upon her,
> they tore her clothes and her flesh,
> they pushed her into the church of Christ,
> and there they finished her. There she died on the floor
>   of the temple."

Dying (her death is a historical moment), Hypatia articulates her attitude toward the god of the Christians. She looks far ahead into the future; her eyes are open to the course of the world. In two lines George sums up the knowledge of the inevitable direction of history—knowledge that they all have already comprehended:

> "In this way the dream of Hellenic Reason ended
> In this way, on the floor of Christ."

Luzi interprets Hypatia's death in Christian terms. Hypatia stands very close to Christ, and her sacrifice becomes a martyrdom. The fanatics who murder her are not the evil Christians portrayed by Kingsley, but the ever-present powers of evil and crime inherent in any crowd. The defining structures and concepts of Christian Europe have burgeoned from the soil of the Alexandrian convulsions and dramas, from Hypatia's sacrifice, from fanaticism and despair. Christian Europe is the consummation of the ancient world. Luzi's drama enriches the thin tradition of Hypatia's presence in Christian literature.

Hypatia appears as a character in other contemporary literature, either in works devoted to her or in novels set in the late Roman empire.[24] In Germany Arnulf Zitelmann's recent historical novel *Hypatia* has been a great popular success.[25] Zitelmann's Hypatia remains a pagan to the end. Intending to found a Platonic state behind the Pillars of Hercules, she journeys to Athens and visits Plutarch, the head of the Platonic Academy; subsequently she travels to Delphi, Dodona, Nicopolis, and Phaistos on Crete. After returning to Alexandria, she delivers a speech in the forum directed against Cyril and his supporters. She is murdered by monks in the company of a Christian mob. Zitelmann describes the event in what are by now familiar terms: the book abounds in descriptions of the perfidiousness, greed, and obscurantism of the church. In the epilogue he repeats the claim made by others: "The attack on Hypatia marks the end of antiquity." He adds: "Hypatia, the daughter of Theon, was the first martyr to that misogyny which later rose to a frenzy in witch hunts."

Canada, too, has produced two novels about Hypatia, André Ferretti's *Renaissance en Paganie* (Montreal, 1987) and Jean

Marcel's *Hypatie ou la fin des dieux* (Montreal, 1989).[26] Both express viewpoints close to those of Kingsley and Zitelmann.

The latest development in the legend of Hypatia concerns her appeal to feminists. Two scholarly feminist journals have taken her name: *Hypatia: Feminist Studies,* published in Athens since 1984; and *Hypatia: A Journal of Feminist Philosophy,* published at Indiana University since 1986. In 1989 the latter featured a vivid poetic prose portrait of the life and death of Hypatia as seen through the eyes of feminist poet and novelist Ursula Molinaro.[27] The introduction to the text reiterates a theme voiced earlier in Claudio Pascal: "The torture killing of the noted philosopher Hypatia by a mob of Christians in Alexandria in 415 A.D. marks the end of a time when women were still appreciated for the brain under their hair."

In Molinaro's account Hypatia's father, Theon, has been warned by the stars about the approaching martyrdom of his daughter. We learn that while still an adolescent, but already famous as a philosopher, she commenced taking lovers and then married the philosopher Isidore, who tolerated his wife's "many amorous friendships." The same stars that had granted Hypatia power over men also divined her tragic death. Aware of his daughter's doom, Theon wants her to move to Sicily, the ancient seat of Greek philosophers, but she rejects the suggestion. She wants to continue to teach her students, among them Synesius. Besides, Hypatia senses the passing of the epoch in which women are permitted to think and to achieve a level of erudition that makes them superior to men; she herself is superior to her father and her husband, Isidore. Moreover, she does not want to leave behind her current lover, the prefect Orestes.

The rumor circulates in Alexandria that Hypatia has formed an alliance with the pagan Orestes against the patriarch Cyril. Cyril incites the faithful and his supporters, headed by Peter the Reader, to rebel against Hypatia. The patriarch begrudges Hypatia her success, and he cannot condone the "adulterous conduct of pagan wives." He therefore makes preparations for her death. After describing Hypatia's death at length and in detail,

Molinaro suggests that such will be the lot of women in Christian times, in which Hypatia "had no desire to live." Subsequently Hypatia's murderers (Christians) constrained all free thought and offered women "a new role model of depleasurized submission."

Through its arbitrariness, fabrications, and alterations Molinaro's text goes considerably beyond previous literary mythologizing seeking to justify through Hypatia various perspectives on history, religion, and Greek antiquity.

Hypatia has also been commemorated in feminist art. In the controversial sculptural work of the feminist artist Judy Chicago exhibited in the San Francisco Museum of Modern Art in 1979, Hypatia is presented as a participant—together with other famous and talented women of Western civilization—at a dinner party that dazzles by its sheer size (but not elegance).[28]

The Origins of the Legend

Few ancient sources underlie the literary tradition about the beautiful young Hypatia, famous philosopher and mathematician, admired by her fellow pagans and despised by Christians, especially by the patriarch Cyril, who with his people delivered her to an undeserved and cruel death, and so on, and so forth—rehearsed in diverse variations.

A few rudimentary elements of the legend originate in Socrates Scholasticus' fifth-century ecclesiastical history. Socrates not only waxes eloquent about Hypatia's virtues, her erudition, and her popularity in the city; he also provides the most detailed description of her murder, including the name of the leader of the band that killed her: Peter, who is mentioned in almost all subsequent narratives about Hypatia. Here is part of Socrates' account:

> It was at that time that envy arose against this woman. She happened to spend a great deal of the time with Orestes, and that stirred up slander against her among people of the Church, as if she were one who prevented Orestes from entering into friend-

ship with the Bishop. Indeed, a number of men who heatedly reached the same conclusion, whom a certain Peter (who was employed as a reader) led, kept watch for the woman as she was returning from somewhere. They threw her out of her carriage and dragged her to the church called Caesarion. They stripped off her clothes and then killed her with broken bits of pottery [*ostraka*]. When they had torn her body apart limb from limb, they took it to a place called Cinaron and burned it.[29]

Socrates, however, leaves open the question of Cyril's complicity in the crime.

The only clear and unequivocal accusation of the patriarch and the Alexandrian Christians occurs in Damascius' *Life of Isidore*.[30] Before the reconstruction and separate publication of this work, the following fragment was preserved as the entry on Hypatia in *Suda*. According to this account, Cyril sought the fulfillment of his ambition by having Hypatia murdered, and his bestial supporters performed the deed and went unpunished. The crime is described as a street scene in which the patriarch himself is a participant:

> Cyril, the bishop of the opposing party, went by Hypatia's house and noticed a great throng at her door, "a jumble of steeds and men." Some came, some went; others remained standing. He asked what this gathering meant and why such a tumult was being made. He then heard from his retainers that the philosopher Hypatia was being greeted and that this was her house. This information so pierced his heart that he launched a murderous attack in the most detestable manner. For when Hypatia was going out as usual, several bestial men, fearing neither divine vengeance nor human punishment, suddenly rushed upon her and killed her: thus laying their country both under the highest infamy and under the guilt of innocent blood. And indeed the Emperor was grievously offended at this matter, and the murderers had been certainly punished, but that Aedesius did corrupt the Emperor's friend: so that his Majesty it is true remitted the punishment but drew vengeance on himself and posterity, his nephew paying dearly for this action.

Writers of the eighteenth and nineteenth centuries found this version of the murder of the pagan philosopher in popular histories of the church as well as in widely known and highly esteemed histories of antiquity such as those of Sébastien Le Nain de Tillemont or Edward Gibbon. Gibbon's description of the events of 415 well served those who wanted to portray the disappearance of Greek civilization as well as those who wished to tarnish the relatively new and rising church. About Cyril, the Alexandrian church, and Hypatia, Gibbon wrote:

> He [Cyril] soon prompted, or accepted, the sacrifice of a virgin who professed the religion of the Greeks ... Hypatia, the daughter of Theon the mathematician, was initiated in her father's studies; her learned comments have elucidated the geometry of Apollonius and Diophantus, and she publicly taught, both at Athens and Alexandria, the philosophy of Plato and Aristotle. In the bloom of beauty, and in the maturity of wisdom, the modest maid refused her lovers and instructed her disciples; the persons most illustrious for their rank or merit were impatient to visit the female philosopher; and Cyril beheld with a jealous eye the gorgeous train of horses and slaves who crowded the door of her academy. A rumour was spread among the Christians that the daughter of Theon was the only obstacle to the reconciliation of the prefect and the archbishop; and that obstacle was speedily removed. On a fatal day, in the holy season of Lent, Hypatia was torn from her chariot, stripped naked, dragged to the church, and inhumanly butchered by the hands of Peter the reader and a troop of savage and merciless fanatics: her flesh was scraped from her bones with sharp oyster-shells, and her quivering limbs were delivered to the flames. The just progress of inquiry and punishment was stopped by seasonable gifts; but the murder of Hypatia has imprinted an indelible stain on the character and religion of Cyril of Alexandria.[31]

In describing Hypatia's fate Gibbon avails himself of both Socrates and *Suda,* but in his anti-Christian fervor he fails to perceive the small yet puzzling fact that Damascius sets the murder of Hypatia on a religious basis. Passing by Hypatia's house, the jealous patriarch Cyril is called "the bishop of the opposing party" *(hairesin)*. We later learn that Damascius has in mind a particular group headed by the bishop. Thus Damascius, who elsewhere in the *Life of Isidore* describes Hypatia's paganism and her teaching of Plato and Aristotle, here places on one level her followers and the Christian environment of the bishop of Alexandria. Does he not therefore treat Hypatia as a person aligned with some Christian movement?

It is possible that Hypatia became affiliated with a Christian creed early in her life, as suggested by a contemporary chronicler of the church, the Arian Philostorgius, who blamed adherents to the Nicene Creed, orthodox Christians, for her death.[32] But Philostorgius' description may be historical intrigue resulting from his steadfast allegiance to Arianism: it is gratifying to blame one's opponents for a crime. So we must seek other clues. They disclose that Damascius may have read texts connecting Hypatia with the theology promulgated by Nestorius.

Diverse authors writing about Hypatia quote a letter of Hypatia's (which is an anonymous fraud) addressed to Cyril, titled "Copy of a letter from Hypatia, who taught philosophy at Alexandria, to the blessed Archbishop Cyril," which contains Hypatia's urgent appeal to Cyril asking him to exercise consideration and understanding for Nestorius and his views on the nature of Christ.[33] Hypatia is thus a presumed Nestorian, that is, a follower of the heresy of Christ's double nature, and "she" writes to Cyril:

> For, as the Evangelist [John 1:18] said, "No one has ever seen God." So how, they say, can you say that God was crucified? They say, too, "How can someone who has not been seen have been fixed to a cross? How could he have died and been buried?" Nestorius, then, who has recently been placed in exile, explained the Apostles' teaching. Now I, who learned long ago that Nestorius himself professed that Christ exists in two natures, say to him who said that, "The gentiles' questions are resolved." There-

fore I say that your holiness did wrong in summoning a synod when you hold views contrary to his and that you contrived in advance that his deposition should take place as a result of the dispute. As for me, after starting this man's exposition a few days ago and comparing the Apostles' teaching, and thinking to myself that it would be good for me to become a Christian, I hope that I may become worthy of the rebirth of baptism.

It is easy to guess the source of the connection between Hypatia and Nestorius. Cyril was a staunch personal opponent of this "heresiarch," as well as of Arianism and Arius' successors. This circumstance probably influenced Philostorgius' account of Hypatia's death, which he attributed to the "homousiasts"—that is, to Cyril and his adherents.

Cyril's differences with Nestorius, his theological and political rival in Constantinople, were fierce and deep. The two patriarchs argued about Christ's divine and human nature, and about Mary. Nestorius referred to her only as the "Mother of Christ" and not as the "Mother of God." Cyril used the contention with Nestorius to promote the cult of Mary in Christian circles, and Nestorius was defeated, condemned at the Council of Ephesus in 431 and declared a heretic. Deprived of his Constantinople patriarchate, he returned to his monastery in Antioch; later "interned" in Egypt, he came under Cyril's rule.

Since the letter mentions Nestorius' banishment, we presume that the fraud—so strangely connected with Hypatia—must have been perpetrated after the Council of Ephesus in 431. It therefore appears that at the close of antiquity there arose a legend linking Hypatia with unorthodox Christianity since two sources—Philostorgius and the anonymous author of the letter to Cyril—seem to have observed her among its sects. At the beginning of the sixth century Damascius showed familiarity with these tendencies in his *Life of Isidore,* an account that was disseminated through *Suda.* Hypatia's association with Christianity persisted, extended by the instigators of the legend of Saint Catherine the Alexandrian, which was constructed on elements drawn from Hypatia's biography. Nor have modern writers hesitated to connect Hypatia with Christianity. Kingsley would have liked to make her a Protestant; Luzi endowed her with a momentous historical mission and linked it to the emergence of Christian Europe from antiquity. The later tradition, however, does not assign her a role in the theological controversies on the nature of divine being.

Eventually, Hypatia returns in the modern literary tradition through a sort of mysterious rebirth of the idea of the past in the poet's soul—an image of Hypatia as Cyril's instructor—in the beautiful poem by Leconte de Lisle. The image persists to our day as we descry it, for example, in Luciano Canfora's book: "celebrated Hypatia who studied geometry and musicology and whom the Christians, convinced in their ignorance that she was a heretic, barbarously murdered in 415."[34]

All works devoted to Hypatia, whether literary, scholarly, or popular, quote an epigram that celebrates the exceptional personal qualities of a woman called Hypatia. Its authorship is connected with the name of an Alexandrian poet of the fourth century, Palladas.[35] He was probably born around 319; thus he was a contemporary of Theon rather than of Hypatia. He lived and wrote when Hypatia was still young, and although we are ignorant of the year of his death, it is difficult to assume that he lived long enough to see Hypatia's death and to know of her achievements. Yet the poem celebrates a person of mature excellence and wisdom elevating her above earthly forms to the stars, to the "heavenly" existence she deserves because of her accomplishments:

> Whenever I look upon you and your words, I pay reverence,
> As I look upon the heavenly home of the virgin.
> For your concerns are directed at the heavens,
> Revered Hypatia, you who are yourself the beauty
>   of reasoning,
> The immaculate star of wise learning.[36]

As G. Luck demonstrates, there is no convincing evidence that the epigram was composed in honor of "our" Hypatia, philosopher and mathematician.[37] Luck believes that it is a poem by an anonymous author addressed to a pious woman named Hypatia, probably the founder of a church ("home of the virgin" in Byzantine poetry refers to a church devoted to Mary). In this reading the walls of the church are decorated with stars and a picture of a woman who is the addressee of the poem. And the poem portrays Hypatia in the context of the constellation Virgo, the astronomical sign of the virgin. Luck's other arguments also appear credible—such as the erroneous identification of Palladas as the poem's author; he was probably confused with another poet, Panolbios.[38] Indeed, in *Suda* we read that Panolbios wrote an epitaph in tribute to Hypatia, the daughter of a high Byzantine official, Erythrius, who in the second half of the fifth century was thrice appointed to the prestigious post of praetorian prefect of the East.[39]

After studying the epigram some scholars, such as Wolfgang Meyer, have inferred that there were two Hypatias: Theon's daughter, at the turn of the fourth and fifth centuries, and Erythrius' daughter, in the second half of the fifth century.[40] This conclusion, however, is only partly correct, for we know that there were more women named Hypatia, including a benefactress of the church in the mid–fifth century (see Sources). The name was by no means uncommon, and it was not confined to pagan women.

Modern historians of the church have taken note of Hypatia. At the beginning of the seventeenth century Caesar Baronius, in his *Annales Ecclesiastici,* wrote ecstatically about her, drawing on a mixture of information from *Suda* and Socrates Scholasticus: "she made such progress in learning that she far surpassed all philosophers of her time"; and he continues: "We can learn from the philosopher Synesius, of whom I have spoken at greater length above, that she shone forth as the most celebrated of all philosophers of that period."[41] Baronius does not explicitly blame Cyril for her death, but he writes with scorn about the Alexandrian church and the bloody event that remains associated with his name.

Toland's perspective on Cyril, however, is foreshadowed by another church historian, G. Arnolds, in his *Kirchen und Ketzer-Historie* (1699).[42] Praising Hypatia's wisdom and ethical perfection, he attributes to Cyril, and the Alexandrian clergy associated with him, criminal intentions toward Hypatia, justified by their struggle to protect the young Christian creed. Arnolds describes Cyril's relentlessness toward theologians promulgating views in conflict with those officially endorsed, and his methods in the struggle to preserve the Nicene orthodoxy.

Le Nain de Tillemont—the historian of antiquity and the church who was most esteemed by Gibbon—also writes about Hypatia.[43] He too dissolves in praise of Hypatia's soul, character, and ascetic and virginal life. Describing her achievements, he asserts that in her own time she was a widely known and respected philosopher. By proclaiming that she was teaching philosophy in Athens and Alexandria, enjoying great respect in both cities, he makes the same error repeated by Gibbon later. Like other contemporary historians, he confuses fact and fiction when writing about Hypatia; he condemns Cyril but at the same time conjectures about the real perpetrators of the murder; he gullibly relies on *Suda,* but he also questions its data.

Johann Albert Fabricius likewise relies on *Suda,* repeating the tale invented by Hesychius, and preserved in *Suda,* that Hypatia was married to the philosopher Isidore.[44] He also disseminates the view that Hypatia was a worshiper of pagan gods, a philosopher devoted to pagan culture. He is equivocal in his assessment of the events connected with her death, although he describes Cyril as "a headstrong and arrogant man."

The first treatise on Hypatia with scholarly aspirations appeared as early as 1689,[45] followed sixty years later by J. C. Wernsdorff's dissertation.[46] But not until the second half of the nineteenth century, with improved critical methods of studying antiquity, did more substantial works on Hypatia appear. In 1860

R. Hoche collected all the primary material on Hypatia then known, in an article titled "Hypatia die Tochter Theons." This was followed by three small monographs: a biography by Stephan Wolf, *Hypatia die Philosophin von Alexandrien* (1879); Hermann Ligier's *De Hypatia philosopha et eclectismi Alexandrini fine* (1879); and Wolfgang A. Meyer's *Hypatia von Alexandrien. Ein Beitrag zur Geschichte des Neuplatonismus* (1886). All three monographs, however, reflect Romantic and neo-Hellenic influences and are uncritically admiring, characterizing Hypatia as a heroically wise and great Hellenic woman. Like contemporary fictional accounts, they contain long descriptions of Hypatia's death, with the patriarch Cyril as the chief instrument.

The same account and accusations persist today in historical studies of Hypatia, in various kinds of dictionaries and encyclopedias, in histories of mathematics, and in works dealing with women's contributions to the history of science and philosophy. Thus, the *Dictionary of Scientific Biography* (1972) characterizes her as "the first woman in history to have lectured and written critical works on the most advanced mathematics of her day." A. W. Richeson, writing about "the celebrated mathematician–philosopher Hypatia," asserts that after her death "we have no other mathematician of importance until late in the Middle Ages."[47] Similarly, R. Jacobacci states that "with her passing there was no other woman mathematician of importance until the eighteenth century."[48] M. Alic describes Hypatia as the most eminent woman scientist before Marie Curie.[49] B. L. Van der Waerden reiterates the theme that Alexandrian science ceased with her death: "Hypatia, a very learned woman, heroine of romantic atrocity tales. She was handsome, she was eloquent, she was charming, she wrote learned commentaries on Diophantus and on Apollonius . . . After Hypatia, Alexandrian mathematics came to an end."[50]

And now Hypatia has been incorporated into the political, social, and cultural history of Africa. B. Lumpkin assumes that Hypatia, "one of the universal geniuses of antiquity," "the last great woman scientist of antiquity," and "woman algebraist, martyr to science," must have been African, not Greek, because of the way she conducted herself: her appearing in public places, her unrestrained behavior and speech.[51] And M. Bernal, writing about Afro-Asian sources of classical civilization, asserts: "Twenty-five years later [after the destruction of the Serapis temple] the brilliant and beautiful philosopher and mathematician Hypatia was gruesomely murdered in the same city by a gang of monks instigated by St. Cyril. These two acts of violence mark the end of Egypto-Paganism and the beginning of the Christian Dark Ages."[52]

⌣ II ⌣

HYPATIA
AND HER
CIRCLE

Clearly, it is impossible to recreate the life and achievements of Hypatia by relying on the literary legend. Exercising the prerogatives of artistic license, poets, novelists, and popularizing historians have done little more than multiply subjective images in accordance with their times and personal aims. And however desirable it may be to reexamine Hypatia's life and death in the light of facts, as we shall see in the Sources very little direct evidence about her has survived. However, we know that during the mature period of Hypatia's life her teaching and philosophical activity in Alexandria attracted a considerable number of young people who, impressed by her spiritual and intellectual gifts, accepted her as their master. Thus we can approach Hypatia indirectly, through a survey of her disciples and her teachings.

Disciples

By the early 390s a circle around Hypatia was already firmly established; therefore, it is likely that the circle formed at the end of the 380s. The dearth of ancient sources makes it impossible to identify all Hypatia's students, determine their number or the duration of their studies with her, or assert with certainty the spiritual values and relations that bound them.

The most substantial source on this circle of young luminaries, including the manner in which the group functioned and the nature of Hypatia's teaching, is the correspondence of Synesius of Cyrene.[1] Modern scholars have firmly demonstrated the importance of this material for the recovery of the provincial life of Cyrene as well as various aspects of the political and social history of the late Roman and Byzantine periods.[2] The 156 letters that have survived include epistles to Hypatia herself as well as to Synesius' fellow students during the time of his studies with her. No reminiscences of her by other students—with the minor exception of Damascius—are extant, nor have Hypatia's letters to any of these young men survived. Thus we must be satisfied with what Synesius offers: his letters and occasionally his texts, *Dion, Ad Paeonium de dono,* and *Hymns.*

Synesius' letters acquaint us with his fellow students in varying degrees of familiarity; some, for example, are only mentioned by name. We first meet them at the start of Synesius' studies with Hypatia.

Although the exact chronology of these studies remains elusive—in fact almost all dates for the Cyrenaic are doubtful— we know that he was at Hypatia's school before his departure on an embassy to Constantinople in the 390s to procure tax relief for the province of Pentapolis. According to Alan Cameron, Synesius resided in the capital from autumn 397 until late autumn 400;[3] he would have left Alexandria at least a year before. We therefore conclude that he must have studied in Alexandria from about 390/393 until 395/396.

Synesius returned to Alexandria on several occasions after departing from Constantinople—first for an extensive stay between 401/402 and 404, then in 407, 410, and 411/412.[4] These dates hinge upon Roques's chronology, which differs from that established by other scholars.[5] During those visits he had the opportunity to see his teacher and colleagues who had extended their studies with Hypatia, and to become acquainted with younger students. In his first, extensive stay he may even have resumed his studies with Hypatia. Pursuing them regularly, however, even in a limited way, would have been difficult, because during that time he married and fathered a child. Nevertheless, his contact with Hypatia never ceased. Even as a metropolitan of Pentapolis Synesius retained his admiration and respect for Hypatia, sending her his works and looking forward to letters from her.

Synesius' closest friend and confidant at Hypatia's school was Herculianus, a lover of philosophy and literature.[6] To Synesius he was the "best of men, thrice longed-for of brothers" (*Ep.* 138), and their friendship embodied the Platonic ideal: "He [Plato] fuses those who love one another by his art, so that from being two they become one" (*Ep.* 140). On the basis of the teachings of Plato, Synesius asks Herculianus not to let their relationship be superficial: "If you do not feel all that I feel you do me wrong indeed; but if you do feel all this, it is simple enough. You are only in that case repaying the debt of friendship" (*Ep.* 137).

Except for the information in Synesius' letters, we know nothing about Herculianus, not even his place of origin.[7] In *Epistle* 137 Synesius describes the extraordinary impression made on them both during their earliest meeting with Hypatia, when they first arrived in Alexandria, "away from home." Thus it seems clear that Herculianus came from elsewhere. As Synesius' letters to his friend reveal (*Epp.* 137–146), Herculianus studied in Alexandria for a long time and perhaps remained there for the rest of his life. Clearly, he must have been wealthy to be able to afford expensive studies for many years.[8]

Immediately after his separation from Herculianus, probably sometime between 395 and 397, Synesius experiences a profound need for conversation and spiritual contact with his friend. In *Epistle* 139 he expresses his loneliness and sense of desolation: "May you come to me, friend who are so dear to me! Let us take up again our discourses on philosophy!" In Cyrene he feels torn from the milieu that nurtured his inclinations and spiritual needs: "My city is dear to me because it is my city, but it has become, I know not how, insensible to philosophy. It is therefore not without apprehension that I feel myself alone without help in the absence of one with whom to share my philosophic frenzy!" Under these circumstances the letters passing between Cyrene and Alexandria are filled with reminiscences of the spiritual community in Alexandria. Sometimes only one phrase or sentence from Synesius prompts Herculianus to recall a particular event from their common past. Synesius also reveals a moral obligation imposed on all friends "under the sign of Hypatia": to keep returning in thought and through deed to the meetings with their teacher that illuminated their souls. Hypatia's youthful disciples seek to subordinate their future lives to the same crowning categories and "deeds" of the soul that they shared in Alexandria.

Synesius is enchanted by the letters of his highly erudite friend, and he often assures him that he has been reading them with singular delight. Knowing Herculianus' taste for literature, he sends him samples of his own work (*Epp.* 137, 141). In *Epistle* 143 he mentions having sent twelve iambic poems of his own and four by an unknown earlier author.[9] The *Anthologia Palatina* attributes the latter to Ptolemy,[10] but apparently neither the precocious poet nor Herculianus was aware of their authorship. Synesius probably copied the great mathematician's poems from an unnamed source, or someone had read them to him.

Synesius may also have sent Herculianus his *Cynegetica* (Book on hunting). Apparently he also tried to send it to Hypatia, but it was lost "by certain young men who cared for Hellenism and grace" (*Ep.* 154; also *Ep.* 101). Given Synesius' concern to achieve "grace and harmony of style" (*Ep.* 154) and his admiration for the literary form of Herculianus' letters, we may infer that Hypatia urged her students to be conscientious about form in speech and in writing. Since Synesius interlards his letters to her with quotations from Homer, Aristophanes, and other authors, we can also assume that she had extensive knowledge of Greek literature.

One of the people who carried Herculianus' letters to Synesius was Herculianus' brother Cyrus, mentioned only by name (*Ep.* 146). We do not know whether he too was a student of Hypatia's; we presume, however—following the plausible suggestion of *PRLE*—that he was Fl. Taurus Seleucus Cyrus,[11] a high-ranking official during the reign of Theodosius II and an epic poet of considerable renown, who enjoyed the patronage of the empress Eudocia. He was prefect of Constantinople in 426, praetorian prefect of the East in 439–440, consul in 441, and was admitted to the patriciate. A devout Christian—though for a short time suspected of being a pagan—he became a priest and eventually a bishop of Cotyaeum in Phrygia. Cyrus came from Panopolis, near Thebes; consequently, he is usually referred to as Cyrus of Panopolis in the histories of early Byzantine culture.

If this Cyrus was indeed the brother of our Herculianus, then our assumptions about the latter's wealth, good birth, high connections, and Christianity gain further confirmation. This hypothetical family connection also allows us to conjecture about Herculianus' place of birth: it might have been Panopolis, since Cyrus was born there. This city, with a strong tradition of Greek culture, produced prominent pagans and poets (among them Nonnus and Dioscorus) in the late Hellenistic period.[12] Herculianus' considerably younger brother Cyrus would also have known Hypatia, since he was carrying letters between her disciples during his own student days.

From the same letter (*Ep.* 146) we learn that Herculianus recommended Synesius to the military *comes* (loosely translatable as "count") in Pentapolis, a person whose identity arouses controversy. We do not know his name, but he is mentioned in *Epistles* 142 and 144 to Herculianus, as well as in *Epistles* 98 and 99, addressed to another companion, Olympius. The designation might refer to Paeonius (perhaps *comes Aegypti?*), the addressee of Synesius' letter *Ad Paeonium de dono* (On the gift); or to Simplicius, *comes et magister utriusque militiae per Orientem* in 396–398 and the addressee of *Epistles* 24, 28, and 130.[13] Regardless of the identity of the *comes* in the letters to Herculianus, we may infer with considerable certainty that Herculianus himself was a man with high connections, well acquainted with government and military officials. It is to this influential friend that Synesius recommends Phoebammon, a Cyrenaic neighbor, "a victim of injustice" on whose behalf he asks Herculianus for patronage and intercession (*Ep.* 144). Synesius is confident that Herculianus and his acquaintances in government circles will help this man: "Thanks to the sacred and honored person of Herculianus, he can triumph over his adversaries."

Synesius' beloved "classmate" at Hypatia's school seems to have visited him occasionally in Cyrene. Synesius extends an invitation in *Epistle* 143, and in *Epistles* 144 and 146 he conveys regards from members of his household (old, young, and women).

In *Epistle* 140 Synesius asks Herculianus to convey greetings to Olympius, another schoolmate and student of Hypatia.[14] There are eight surviving letters addressed to Olympius (*Epp.* 44, 96–99, 133, 148, 149), written intermittently between Synesius' return to Cyrenaica and his death. Olympius was a wealthy landowner from Seleucia in Syrian Pieria. Like Herculianus, he remained in Alexandria studying with Hypatia several years longer than Synesius. He probably returned to Syria around 402/403. In *Epistle* 98 Synesius, who is ill, writes Olympius about his nostalgia for Alexandria, where his friend is still living. He expresses longing to revisit the city and to see again the people to whom he feels closest: "If I recover, I am off to Alexandria at once."

The letters passing between Cyrene and Seleucia, after the friends' eventual return to their respective homes, abound with love of philosophy, expressions of friendship, and a taste for the gentry's way of life. *Epistles* 133 and 248 express the pleasure of both in the grace of their rural estates and the aristocratic life style connected with them. Both Synesius and Olympius declare a weakness for horses, dogs, and hunting, as well as delight in leisure for thinking and writing. Synesius describes his estate, about twenty miles from Cyrene, as a place of idyllic bliss. There, the pursuit of philosophy and the pleasures available to members of his class remind him of the "golden age" or "Noe's age," that is, a land of unfathomed happiness (*Ep.* 148). Synesius conveys his zest for life, his delight in exploring eternal creation as manifested in the Libyan rural landscapes. Apparently Olympius visited Synesius in Cyrene; in *Epistle* 99 Synesius sends him greetings from the servants and asks that Olympius relay greetings to his own, especially to "the worthy Abramius," in his house in Alexandria. We do not know whether Synesius ever visited Olympius in Syria; but in *Epistle* 149 he ardently encourages his friend to visit him in Cyrene so that their reunion may revive the spirit of their friendship. There Olympius may have met Synesius' younger brother Euoptius (*Ep.* 114), yet another student of Hypatia's. In the picturesque countryside near Cyrene, the two friends find refuge from the hubbub of the city with its markets and financial operations, which they see as an outrage to the human spirit. They speak of avoiding the struggle for offices, honors, and political careers that gratify only superficial ambitions, and not genuine human values. Synesius, aware that he will never succeed in distancing himself from public life, expresses pleasure in being able to take advantage of quiet periods for reflection: "For us there is time for philosophy, but no time to do evil" (*Ep.* 148).

The friendship between Synesius and Olympius involves exchanges of gifts—horses, bridles, and other lavish presents—as well as of letters. The wealthy Olympius sends so many that Synesius feels embarrassed by their number and magnificence (*Epp.* 133, 149). In moments of danger, however, such as in 405 when desert barbarians threaten his town, Synesius asks his friend to send him not only a good horse but also bows and arrows (*Ep.* 133). His raptures about life in the freshness of nature are not simply literary conventions. When summoned to perform urgent political duties, Synesius reluctantly abandons his leisure in the rural retreat to serve his native polis.

Olympius was undoubtedly a Christian. In 411 Synesius confides to him his doubts and serious perplexities concerning the consecration to bishop offered him by the people of Libyan Ptolemais (*Ep*. 96). In *Epistle* 44, dating from much later, when he was a bishop,[15] he writes about "evil men" who are "troubling our church"—heretics, Eunomians, followers of the anti-Nicene doctrines of Arius. Olympius' faith is so profound that Synesius considers him capable of contending successfully with the Eunomians ("Take steps against them. Only nails drive out nails"). Given that Olympius was a zealous Christian when Synesius was facing a choice between a secular career and a spiritual calling, we may presume that he was already a Christian during his studies with Hypatia.

Olympius was not only well off (*Ep*. 133) but also well connected; in Alexandria he knew the same chief of the imperial armed forces (*Epp*. 98 and 99) whom Herculianus knew. Consequently, Synesius turns also to him for a favor. In *Epistle* 99 he commends to his good graces and protection the poet Theotimus, "the most inspired poet of our times," whom he came to know in Constantinople as a bard eulogizing the virtues of the praetorian prefect Anthemius, "the most powerful minister of Arcadius."[16] Synesius is convinced that under Olympius' patronage the poet, whom he esteems highly, will gain access to "men in high places in Alexandria," and he promises Olympius that the poet will commemorate him for posterity as he has Anthemius (*Ep*. 49).

The letters of Olympius and Herculianus mention the names of other students of Hypatia's. Ision seems to have been a companion of Synesius, Herculianus, and Olympius in her intellectual circle. We know nothing about him, however, except that he visited Synesius in Cyrene and was treated as a member of the household (*Ep*. 144). Writing to Olympius, Synesius refers to him as "your own Ision" (*Ep*. 99), and in a letter to Herculianus he recalls Ision's narrative talent with appreciation

(*Ep.* 144). He appears to have intervened with the authorities on Ision's behalf in some matter.

Equally little is known about several other young men. Syrus, "our friend," carries Synesius' letters to Olympius; and Petrus delivers a letter from Synesius to Hypatia (*Ep.* 133). Both were Syrians, countrymen of Olympius probably studying with Hypatia at his prompting. The name Petrus surely points to his identity as a Christian.

We know even less about yet another fellow student, Hesychius, and the information we have is controversial. From a letter to him from Synesius (*Ep.* 93), some scholars conclude that he was Synesius' compatriot, a wealthy *curialis* of the town of Cyrene; others presume that he did not come from Cyrene but stayed there while on duty as governor of Upper Libya *(dux et corrector Libyarum)* in the first years of the fifth century.[17] However, from *Epistle* 93 we learn that Synesius became acquainted with Hesychius not in Cyrene but at Hypatia's classes in "divine geometry"; so there is good reason to think that Hesychius did not come from Cyrene. It was in Alexandria and not earlier in Cyrene that they became friends, as did Herculianus and Olympius. Is it then possible that Hesychius came from Alexandria or Constantinople? Memories of this friendship and a feeling of brotherhood come to the fore in *Epistle* 93.

Epistle 93 expresses not only friendship for Hesychius but also a grievance; Synesius reproaches him for putting his beloved younger brother Euoptius on the roster of the *curia* in Cyrene (or perhaps only left him on the list?). The incident probably occurred when Synesius was consecrated bishop and had to resign from the town council. As *dux et corrector Libyarum,* Hesychius had the authority to intervene in the affairs of Cyrene; at that time (around 410) he was probably already governor of Upper Libya. After finishing his studies with Hypatia, he may have returned to Constantinople to pursue a prestigious career in the civil service. Having met as Hypatia's students, Hesychius and Synesius came together again years later as eminent and influential men, one an important functionary in the imperial administration, the other a bishop in the Libyan church. *Epistle* 5 reveals that Euoptius was another of Hypatia's students. Apparently he left Cyrene when Hesychius burdened him with curial duties (*Ep.* 93). At that time he may well have gone to Alexandria, for he used to travel there quite frequently, as Synesius' many letters addressed to him there confirm.[18] It is possible that Synesius introduced him into Hypatia's circle during one of his longer visits in Alexandria in the early 400s.[19] In *Epistle* 5 (which Garzya dates to 402 and Roques to 407), Synesius asks Euoptius to convey greetings to "the most holy and revered philosopher" as well as to those who find delight "in her oracular utterances." That Euoptius knew Synesius' fellow students and even studied with some of them is indicated not only by the greetings that Synesius asks him to convey to his Alexandrian friends, but also by his admonition to Hesychius to treat Euoptius like a brother (*Ep.* 93). (Is it then likely that Hesychius studied with Hypatia longer than Synesius, with Euoptius still in Alexandria?) Synesius asks him to behave kindly to Euoptius not only because he is the brother of Hesychius' friend but also because all students of Hypatia's should make up a community loving one another like a family. After all, such conduct tallies with Euclid's geometric principles to which they were introduced by their Alexandrian Mistress, one of which states that two things being equal to the same thing are also equal to one another.[20] Brotherly ties, like those in a family, must be also maintained among friends, separation notwithstanding.

Synesius' brother is the recipient of forty letters making up one third of the entire correspondence. *Epistle* 105, addressed to Euoptius in Alexandria, communicates Synesius' ideological doubts connected with his impending accession to the bishopric. In the letter Synesius consults with Euoptius as if he were his spiritual adviser. Indeed, Euoptius was an ardent Christian and probably succeeded him as bishop of Ptolemais after his brother's death; later he represented Upper Libya at the Council of Ephesus.[21]

At least one other member of Synesius' family also studied

with Hypatia. In *Epistle* 46 he recommends to her his uncle Alexander, his father's brother, as a person worthy of trust. Alexander did indeed study for some time with Hypatia, as we read in *Epistle* 150, dating from about 406. By that time his uncle was dead. Reminiscing about Alexander, Synesius calls him "the philosopher Alexander," adding that during his lifetime he was his friend and commanded widespread respect.

On the other hand, there is no decisive evidence that a childhood friend, a lawyer whose name Synesius does not mention, was one of Hypatia's students.[22] In *Epistle* 47, during his mission in Constantinople, he recommends him to Aurelian, Arcadius' praetorian prefect, whom Synesius immortalized in *On Providence*. Greatly flattering Aurelian, he writes that he wants his former companion in studies to witness the salutary and beneficial effects of the prefect's government.

But there is no doubt that Hypatia's circle included Theotecnus, Athanasius, Theodosius, and Gaius (*Epp.* 5, 16). Synesius only mentions them by name. We know next to nothing about "the worthy and holy Theotecnus."[23] He is probably advanced in years, since Synesius asks Euoptius to extend greetings to "father Theotecnus" (*Ep.* 16) and to "holy father Theotecnus" (*Ep.* 5). Athanasius, as close to Synesius as a brother, is probably the well-known Alexandrian sophist, the author of commentaries and rhetorical works.[24] Theodosius is the Alexandrian "grammarian of the first order" (*Ep.* 5), the author of discourses on verbs and nouns who also made an epitome from Herodian's work on prosody.[25] Nothing can be said about Gaius, whom Synesius describes as "the most sympathetic" man and "a member of our family" (*Ep.* 5). The latter designation need not be taken literally; Synesius is surely referring to Hypatia's circle of students as a family.

According to Garzya, Auxentius was also one of Hypatia's students, Synesius' countryman, and a childhood playmate.[26] In *Epistle* 60 Synesius does indeed remind Auxentius of the years spent together at school and in studies; he asks him to resume contact broken off because of quarrels and misunderstandings with his brother. *Epistle* 117, however, reveals that Auxentius is much younger than Synesius. This circumstance would not prevent us from counting him a student of Hypatia's were it not that he might have been a member of the Cyrenaic cultural circle made up of Synesius' local friends sharing philosophic and creative pursuits. To this circle belonged, for example, Herodes and Martirius, mentioned in *Epistles* 19 and 91.

This brief survey indicates that Hypatia's closest, most loyal students were people who later held high imperial or ecclesiastical positions. Of even greater significance is evidence that agents of the imperial power arriving in Alexandria became close acquaintances of Hypatia and most likely attended her lectures.

Testimony from Damascius supports the notion that Hypatia occupied a strong political and social as well as cultural position in Alexandria. In a rather short and general report, he devotes considerable space to lauding her position in Alexandrian society: with her spiritual standing, political skills, and popularity as a lecturer, he asserts, she promoted respect for philosophy and commanded the esteem of Alexandria's chief politicians for her principles. Accordingly, high officials *(archontes)* who assumed the burden of public responsibilities in Alexandria paid early calls on Hypatia as one of the foremost people in the city.[27] In this respect, Damascius says, Alexandria at this time resembled fifth-century B.C. Athens, where politicians used to call on famous philosophers to elicit advice on matters of state.

One auditor at Hypatia's widely attended public lectures was undoubtedly Orestes, augustal prefect in Alexandria, civil governor of Egypt in the years 412(?)–415, and a key figure in the incidents connected with Hypatia's death.[28] Our best informant, Socrates Scholasticus, tells us unequivocally that Hypatia and Orestes knew each other well and met frequently, and that he consulted with her on municipal and political issues.[29] He also supplies the highly interesting news that Orestes was a Christian, having been baptized in Constantinople by the patriarch Atticus before his appointment as governor of Egypt.[30] The disclosure is confirmed by John of Nikiu, known for his enmity toward

Hypatia. After noting that under the influence of Hypatia's evil magic practices Orestes "ceased attending church *as had been his custom*" (emphasis added), he observes that Orestes "honored her exceedingly."[31] Socrates sought her advice with such confidence that he was regarded as entirely under the influence of her hostility toward the patriarch Cyril and the policy of the Alexandrian church.

So in all probability Orestes, after arrival in Alexandria, and following the example of others, especially that of local civil servants, paid Hypatia a visit, became acquainted, and attended her lectures. Thus he at once satisfied his intellectual interests and deferred to good manners: it simply behooved officials and civil servants who became Hypatia's friends and elicited her advice to attend her lectures.[32]

Hypatia's interlocutors and auditors may also have included the military *comes* mentioned in Synesius' letters to Herculianus and Olympius.[33] This figure may have been Simplicius, who was *magister militum per Orientem* (commander in chief in the East) in the years 396–398 and *magister militum praesentalis* (commander of central field armies) in 405. We do not know whether he attended Hypatia's lectures while Synesius was studying in Alexandria. *Epistle* 146, addressed to Herculianus after Synesius' departure from the city, indicates that the *comes* Simplicius was not well known to Synesius. He must have resided in the city for some time, though, since the two letters in which Synesius mentions a *comes* (*Epp.* 98, 144) were sent to Alexandria. Perhaps Simplicius lived in Alexandria temporarily or visited it between his military assignments. Maybe he stayed there earlier, shortly before Synesius' departure from Alexandria around 396. In any case, his acquaintance with three leading students of Hypatia's makes it reasonable to assume that he was connected with the circle of young philosophers associated with Hypatia. This inference is strengthened by Synesius' praise of his intellectual cultivation (*Ep.* 142).

If Synesius did not meet Simplicius in Alexandria, then he might have seen him in Pentapolis. We know that Simplicius was directing a military reform in Pentapolis and paid frequent visits there; for Simplicius came from Pentapolis. In any case, in *Epistle* 24 Synesius calls himself an "old" friend of Simplicius; in other letters (for example, *Ep.* 134) he recalls meetings and hunting with him.

Among civil servants, the *archontes* calling on Hypatia may also have included Pentadius and Heliodorus. Pentadius, who is the addressee of two letters from Synesius (*Epp.* 29 and 30), was augustal prefect of Egypt in 403–404 (at which time Synesius was most probably again in Alexandria).[34] He held the same high post in Egypt that was later bestowed on Orestes. In *Epistle* 30 Synesius, praising Pentadius, writes that his just and benevolent conduct results from his enchantment with Platonian philosophy; and in *Epistle* 127 he calls him "the most amiable and cultivated man." It is therefore possible that he, too, was for a time Hypatia's student or at least attended her open lectures for a wider public, mentioned by Damascius. The lectures were most likely frequented by educated individuals: members of the local council, persons appointed for temporary civil service in Alexandria, or high state officials stopping there for a few days.

There is insufficient documentary evidence that Heliodorus was a student of Hypatia's or attended her lectures. According to some scholars, he was a rhetorician and lawyer at the court of the Egyptian augustal prefect in Alexandria;[35] Roques suggests that he was civil governor of Pentapolis in the years 405–410.[36] Speculations aside, there is no doubt that he came from Alexandria and was a close acquaintance of the prefect's. The fact that Synesius asks him for a recommendation to the prefect of Egypt on behalf of his lawyer friend bespeaks Heliodorus' high rank (*Ep.* 116). Elsewhere (*Ep.* 17) Synesius describes him as highly educated and endowed with impressive oratorical skill and a sublime soul. These characteristics surely qualified Heliodorus for inclusion in Hypatia's group of friends.

Finally, one of Hypatia's students may have been Ammonius, the only Alexandrian *curialis* or councilor known by name, who appears in four of Synesius' letters (*Epp.* 18–21) and of whom Synesius speaks with great affection and respect. Like his colleagues on the council, he was not only acquainted with Hypatia; he also attended her lectures. Moreover, Synesius' letters indicate that he was deeply interested in people associated with the woman philosopher.

Socrates, whose *Ecclesiastical History* is our most substantial source, testifies to Hypatia's position in Alexandria: "On account of the majestic outspokenness at her command as the result of her education, she maintained a dignified intercourse with the chief people of the city, for all esteemed her highly, and admired her for her sophrosyne." Moving in high government circles, surrounded by imperial and town dignitaries and by wealthy, well-born, and influential students, Hypatia must have had some voice in town affairs and have influenced political and social life in Alexandria. It is therefore not surprising that Synesius, himself a person of distinction acquainted with many notables in the administrative and government circles at court in Constantinople, turned to her for recommendations that people in power took seriously. Thus he asks her to aid two young men from Cyrene, Nicaeus and Philolaus, who lost their estates because of sordid schemes against them (*Ep.* 81). Aware of her connections and informed of her position in Alexandria, Synesius prompts her to intervene on behalf of the victims with her influential and powerful acquaintances, private as well as official *(kai idiotais kai archousi).*

It is worth noting in this connection that in *Epistle* 80 Synesius also asks the bishop Theophilus to intercede with higher authorities on behalf of one of the young men, Nicaeus. Apparently, the chief representative of Greek culture in the city and the head of the church enjoyed similar influence and operated in the same spheres. In social prestige there was no significant difference between the patriarch and the woman teacher of philosophy. Both were asked in this case to assist individuals with a common background—Christians brought up in the Greek *paideia*. What is more, Synesius regards Hypatia and Theophilus on equal terms; addressing them in *Epistles* 5, 105, and 12, he applies the same rhetorical embellishment.

Bearing in mind Hypatia's unique position in Alexandria, we should not be surprised by some scholars' assumption that among her listeners there might have been priests or candidates to the priesthood. There is justification for this assumption, since from the times of Ammonius, precursor of Plotinian thought, Alexandrian schools did not separate students on religious grounds. Pagan pupils attended classes of Christian teachers, Christian ones those of pagan teachers.[37] The assumption has been supported by the fact that Synesius and the future church father Isidore of Pelusium were studying in Alexandria at the same time. Isidore was presbyter (he may have been the abbot) of the convent in Pelusium near present-day Port Said.[38] It seems plausible that he was a member of the student circle around Hypatia. But Synesius never speaks directly about Isidore; he does not mention him in any of his writings.

Isidore's correspondence, however, includes four letters addressed to a certain "Synesiōi." This fact indicates to Crawford,[39] for example, that Synesius knew Isidore and consulted him on ecclesiastical matters. Lacombrade holds the same opinion, suggesting that they were friends in Hypatia's circle, that in time Isidore even became to Synesius a sort of moral tutor.[40] Garzya likewise thinks that Isidore was one of Synesius' triad of friends described in *Epistle* 143. Together with Synesius, during their studies with Hypatia, they formed a "foursome" elected by fortune.[41]

All these suppositions, however, are based on only one, though highly suggestive, sentence in *Epistle* 144. In it Synesius asks Herculianus to salute his "holy comrade the deacon." Indeed, the friends in Hypatia's circle referred to one another as *hetairoi,* companions, which may be taken as an argument in favor of Lacombrade's and Garzya's thesis. But the absence of the "deacon's" name raises doubts; we have no letter from Synesius to Isidore; and Isidore in his abundant correspondence does not mention studying with Hypatia, nor do the sources recounting his life. Surely, the thought-provoking information that this orthodox and austere church father studied with a "pagan" woman philosopher would have survived in the historiographic tradition if there were only a trace of it in the sources.

Its absence might be explained by the contemporary authors' practice of omitting detailed biographical data about the figures described, which Synesius does himself with regard to both Hypatia and his former fellow students, making study of Hypatia's milieu difficult. The circumstance, of course, does not change the fact that we still lack assurance about Isidore's association with Hypatia's school and the narrow circle of her pupils. Even Crawford's enticing hypothesis on the existence of letters from Isidore to Synesius, together with his enumeration of terminological and literary similarities in the epistolary collections of both men of the church,[42] hardly authenticates Lacombrade's and Garzya's suppositions. G. Redl rightly remarks that the similarity of thought and formulations, the quoting of the same Greek authors, and the use of topoi from the exegetical writings flows from the type of education both luminaries received in Greek and Christian schools, rather than from their association with each other.[43]

Isidore, who lived in approximately 360–434, was probably educated in Alexandria (which may have been his place of birth). Though brought up as a Christian, he received a classical education not unlike that of young non-Christians of his age. It is therefore conceivable that Isidore attended Hypatia's lectures, just as Synesius could have attended the Alexandrian catechetical school (and most likely did). Given the nature of Isidore's correspondence and his profound faith in the Christian religion, however, it is difficult to accept the thought that he was a faithful and devoted student of Hypatia's. Still, we are certain that the monk Isidore knew Euoptius, Synesius' brother; one of his epistles is addressed to him.[44] Isidore, however, came to know Euoptius only as a bishop, which means that they became acquainted after Synesius' death.

Speculations aside, our reflections on possible ties between St. Isidore, Synesius, and the circle of Greek luminaries around Hypatia lead to one unambiguous conclusion: Hypatia's circle included a "deacon," an ecclesiastic, who was undoubtedly a companion of Herculianus, Synesius, and perhaps Olympius or even Hesychius. He might have become their friend in Hypatia's circle or outside it while visiting ecclesiastical institutions of Alexandria. They may have met him at the catechetical school, or through acquaintances connected with the bishop Theophilus, who entertained close relations with Synesius and probably with his friends. The term *hetairos* in Synesius' letters is not confined to the characterization of philosopher friends or lay persons. In *Epistle* 105 he refers to the bishops Paulus and Dionysius as *hetairoi* of the patriarch Theophilus.

This "deacon" closes the roster of young men who, bound by friendship, studied with Hypatia. Our meager sources provide all too few data about them. But their diverse places of origin do much to confirm the testimony of our chief historian, Socrates Scholasticus, to the effect that "everyone who wanted to study philosophy flocked to her from all directions." They came from Cyrene, Syria, and Alexandria, from the Thebaid, and from the capital of the empire, sharing a similar background, wealth, and ties with the world of the rulers. They draw our attention not only because of these attributes, but also on account of more striking characteristics. Around this "last woman pagan," "woman Hellenic-martyr," and "victim of appalling Christian fanaticism" (as some makers of her modern legend would have her) gathered Christians, pagan sympathizers, and future converts. Two even became bishops. Although we lack information about the ideological and biographical courses of others in her circle, that Christians were attracted to Hypatia is confirmed even by John of Nikiu, who writes that the Christian Orestes "drew many believers to her."[45]

Contrary, however, to what John of Nikiu would like us to believe (for his message obviously refers to Hypatia's anti-Christian stance), no source even implies that under the influence of this "obdurate pagan" any of her students yielded to apostasy or, perturbed by her anti-Christian views, wanted to annihilate her person and teaching.[46] She was, we remember, capable of helping people who were seeking the patriarch Theophilus' protection; she maintained close relations with the civil servants of the town and the empire, in their majority already Christians.

Membership in a circle with such a spiritual formation answers many questions about the life of its most illustrious member, Synesius, as well as about that of his brother Euoptius. In his study Cameron rightly argues that Synesius had strong ties with Christianity at home and during his "Alexandrian" youth, as well as in maturity.[47] He substantiates this thesis with material from Synesius' writings (above all, from the hymns and letters), with events from his personal life, and with the ideas prevalent in the intellectual milieu in which he lived. A statement in *Epistle* 8, addressed to his brother, the future bishop, suggests that both were brought up in the Christian faith: "Let alone the fact that we are born of the same parents, we were brought up together, and we have our education in common." If they had not received education in the faith at home and sustained it throughout their years of studies in Alexandria, how could both brothers, descended from a pagan family, have become bishops?

Nurtured in the Greek *paideia*, Synesius could in his association with Hypatia develop his religious urges and needs, thanks to the spiritualism of Late Platonic philosophy in which she educated her disciples. Given the openness and spiritual opportunities of the milieu, it is not surprising that this student of Hypatia's (like his brother) ended his life as a bishop. Neither should we be astonished by the fact that in Alexandria, the place of his "pagan" education, shortly after finishing his studies with Hypatia, he married a Christian with the patriarch Theophilus' blessing. Around that time (that is, in the early 400s) he was baptized, either in Cyrene or in Alexandria. Finally, in Alexandria between 410 and 412 he was consecrated—also by Theophilus—bishop of the town Ptolemais in his native Upper Libya.[48] Thus, close association with Hypatia did not prevent Synesius from strengthening his ties with Christianity (both in Alexandria and in Cyrene); just as spiritual rapport with Theophilus, a Christian marriage, baptism, and a growing affirmation of his faith did not alter his attitude toward his woman teacher. *Epistle* 154, his longest letter to Hypatia, dates from the end of 404 or 405, its affectionate tone apparently undiminished by his recently established association with the church.

The reborn and deepened religiosity of the student did not change the teacher's attitude toward him. Neither do we notice that his close affiliation with Hypatia provoked any conflicts with Bishop Theophilus. Despite Synesius' theological doubts stemming from his obsession with philosophy, he was never censored by Theophilus, who strongly seconded him to the bishopric. During his tenure as bishop Synesius maintained a lively correspondence with Theophilus (*Epp.* 9, 66–69, 76, 80, 90) while writing letters to Hypatia filled with devotion and admiration and expressing longing for intellectual contact with her. Neither is there any indication in the sources of conflict between Hypatia and the bishop of Alexandria, Synesius' patron.[49] Esteemed by the ruling elite, sympathetic toward Christians, indifferent to pagan cults, neutral in the religious fights and altercations, she lived in Alexandria for many years enjoying the city's rulers' respect and her disciples' love.

In Pursuit of Knowledge

After his departure from Alexandria and between later visits to the city, Synesius wrote at least seven letters to his spiritual mentor and friend (*Epp.* 10, 15, 16, 46, 81, 124, 154), addressed to "Hypatia, the philosopher." Most are brief and principally about his own experiences and indispositions. We learn little from them about Hypatia's life. A close reading of Synesius' letters, however, yields some facts and historical perceptions. *Epistle* 81, for example, discloses valuable information about Hypatia as protectress, and the longest—*Epistle* 154—presents her as a critic evaluating Synesius' work. All are marked by deep emotion. Synesius remains bound to the memory of his studies with her. His admiration appears to have been permanent.

Together with his letters to Herculianus, Synesius' letters to Hypatia provide a valuable source for the reconstruction of occurrences in Hypatia's "school." Those to Herculianus flesh out the substance of the philosophic sessions with her and reveal a profound fascination with Hypatia.

Synesius describes their lecturer as a "blessed lady" (*Ep.* 10). According to his letters and Socrates Scholasticus' report, she radiates knowledge and wisdom derived from "divine" Plato himself and his successor Plotinus. Through them she possesses the gift of communicating with the divine mystery, which inclines students to attribute to her the "sainthood" that Synesius, in all his writings, bestows on Plato, as do all Neoplatonic philosophers of the period; they regard him as the indisputable master of philosophy and knowledge about the world of divine forms.[50]

Thus Hypatia's students always feel the presence of her "divine spirit."[51] Not just Hypatia's soul is holy; all of her being is sanctified; even her hands, which receive Synesius' letters, are "sacred" (*Ep.* 133). As Plato's successor she is blessed with charisma that enables her to teach others, and she fulfills her vocation with devotion, as if god himself had called her to this purpose. Zealously disclosing to her students the "sacred" sense of philosophic inquiry, she is regarded as a "genuine guide in the mysteries of philosophy" *(gnesia kathegemon ton philosophias orgion)* (*Ep.* 137). The appellation of guide along the avenues of "genuine" sacred philosophy was accorded in Hypatia's time only to those Neoplatonists who distinguished themselves through a sort of personal holiness, through fame on account of their wisdom and spiritual authority.[52] At the side of so elevated a teacher students consider themselves Fortune's darlings. They surround her joyfully, like choristers their leader. Writing in 402 to his brother Euoptius, who was probably still studying with Hypatia, Synesius asks him to extend salutations to "the fortunate chorus that delights in her oracular utterance," or more precisely "in her divinely sweet voice" (*Ep.* 5).

Plato once spoke in like voice (*Ep.* 140), and students surrounding masters of Late Platonism in the fourth century compared themselves to a chorus. The same metaphoric language was used by Libanius to describe the circle of disciples in Syrian Apamaea surrounding Iamblichus, who is referred to as the leader of a chorus of souls "gathered to the gods."[53] Now, several decades later in Alexandria, the most venerable woman philosopher, Hypatia beloved by the gods (*Ep.* 5), continues the tradition of Late Platonism, for she teaches her students to regard philosophy as a kind of religious mystery, "the most ineffable of ineffable things" (*Ep.* 137). She calls up their philosophic instinct, extricates religious images and feelings directed toward divine reality.

The "genuine guide" who presides over the mysteries of philosophy commands her disciples to follow Plato's teachings, and through a strenuous effort of mind and heart to extract from their inner selves "the eye buried within us" (*Ep.* 137).[54] This "intellectual eye," that "luminous child of reason" (*Ep.* 139; *Dion* 9) hidden deep inside us waiting for release, renders the individual a bearer of the transcendental world, making him capable of bursting the shackles of matter. In this common effort of discovering the natural resources of human divinity, Hypatia was probably admonishing her students to heed Plotinus' words on his deathbed. Synesius quotes them to his friend Herculianus: "Raise up the divine within you to the first-born divine" (*Ep.* 139).[55]

The spark of wisdom kindled by the "divine guide," that "hidden spark which loves to conceal itself," turns into a large flame of cognition (*Ep.* 139), thus concluding the journey of the soul which Plotinus termed *anagoge,* the ascension toward heaven, toward divinity.[56] The goal of philosophizing is achieved; the mind is in a state of revelation, contemplation, *theoria* (*Ep.* 140; *Dion* 6–9).[57] This is the consummate experience, incontrovertible, for it touches on prime being, true reality, the original cause of temporal reality. This indeed is the most important realm in human life: "to be given over to the things above and entirely to the contemplation of Reality and the origin of mortal things" (*Ep.* 140).

The person who experiences this singular event makes a radical turn in life (*Ep.* 143), attains the "true life" (*Ep.* 137) so much sought after by every philosopher. From now on this true life will be always subordinated to reason, to using its cognitive tools to seek eternal wisdom first, later to submitting to ecstasy to elevate oneself into another dimension of existence and to direct merging with the One. The happiness of merging with this Being, which Synesius likes to call "first-born divine," is so great that all Hypatia's students want the state to last for as long as possible: "I should wish it to be a property of our nature to be always lifted up toward contemplation" (*Dion* 8).

The mind, bent to the light, contemplates ultimate Beauty and Goodness, and not the contrived, shifting, and ephemeral beauty and goodness that man beholds in the material order of existence. But achieving this elevation of the mind in agreement with Plato's teaching hinges on the development of cognitive powers throughout one's life. "Life lived according to reason is the end of men. Let us pursue that life; let us ask for divine wisdom from God" (*Ep.* 137). The aim and sense of philosophy understood as "the most ineffable of ineffable things" becomes intelligible for Hypatia's students initiated into its rites. What so far has been ineffable for them becomes unraveled. Hypatia's teachings on the search for the "mystery of being" was not lost on Synesius. Throughout his life he pursued contemplation, and his most accomplished works—the *Hymns*—are an emphatic confirmation of the pursuit. Exceedingly burdened with the duties of a bishop, he always looked back to his youth, filled with studies and contemplation, as a period of highest happiness, "I who have devoted my youth to philosophical leisure and to the contemplation of abstract being" (*Ep.* 11). In moments filled with ecclesiastical responsibilities he did not hesitate to affirm that it was precisely *theoria* that he considered to be the purpose of his priesthood: "Contemplation is the end and aim of the priesthood" (*Ep.* 41).

The wisdom that commands man to recognize and understand only divine things and that compels him to the search for the indefinite and the mysterious also raises him above bodily perfection. Man's elevation beyond his body means that in his search for god he remains free of affections, he lives in harmony with himself, indifferent to the things of the world. Consequently, the course along which Hypatia was leading her disciples to that which they called "the union with the divine" required both vast cognitive effort and ethical perfection. Wisdom alone was not sufficient. Hypatia taught them that to gain this insight, which is located on the fringes of knowledge, which recognizes only beauty, they must be beautiful themselves; they must be perfect. Our sources reveal that she did not hesitate to apply harsh pedagogical measures to students who did not want to comprehend this basic truth.

Damascius tells of such an instance. He relates a story carried away from Hypatia's school, which possibly includes her own words—if so, this fragment represents an extraordinary rarity. According to Damascius' report, one of Hypatia's regular students fell in love with her. Unable to control his feelings, the young man confessed his love. Hypatia resolved to punish him, and she found an effective method of chasing him away. As a symbol of the female body's physicality she showed him her sanitary napkin, remonstrating: "This is what you really love, my young man, but you do not love beauty for its own sake."[58]

Damascius relates the incident in another version, in which Hypatia is said to have prevailed over the young man's passion through music.[59] But Damascius himself judged the version "ignorant," and he was probably right; it was probably introduced for the sole purpose of softening the ugliness of the authentic story. Cameron is correct when he states that this alternate version put Hypatia in a more favorable light, but he is wrong when he maintains that it fitted her better as a Platonist.[60] The vulgar story is in fact profoundly Platonic; it displays to us the true character of the woman. It shows Hypatia's repugnance toward the human body and sensuality. She certainly was not endowed with an enticing, pleasing, or sympathetic personality. Such qualities do not fit her. One might say about Hypatia—and the sources do—that she was endowed with uncommon force of character and ethical fortitude.

The interpretation of this incident requires no complicated reasoning.[61] Those who recall Socrates' rejection of Alcibiades' wooing find Hypatia's conduct easy to explain. Hypatia's revolting act was intended to make the student understand the deeper meaning of Eros and to "turn" him in that direction. During her lectures she devoted much effort to speaking about that "eye buried within us" in order to make the student capable of applying the acquired knowledge. Since the young man, despite being her student, showed complete ignorance, she violated him psychologically (whereas Socrates only derided Alcibiades' stupidity) to make him see that beauty cannot be identified with a concrete object (in this case Hypatia's body).[62] Her perception of Eros was close to that of Plotinus: "When a man sees the beauty in bodies he must not run after them; we must know that they are images, traces, shadows, and hurry away to that which they image. For if a man runs to the image and wants to seize it as if it was the reality . . . then this man who clings to beautiful bodies and does not let them go . . . sinks down into the dark depths where intellect has no delight, and stays blind in Hades consorting with shadows there and here."[63]

Like Plotinus, she was not interested in beauties that were relative—comely in one aspect, ugly in another. She wanted to unshackle in her students this kind of "delight of intellect" that would lead them to seeing ultimate beauty (*Ep.* 139). Her students were to tear themselves away from the illusoriness and secondariness of the world; they were to substitute true recognition for supposition, and to ignore, forget, objects such as "beautiful people." Her young student got so used to the world of suppositions that Hypatia felt compelled to apply a revolting measure to shock his will, reason, and moral sense.

Indeed, she achieved what she was aiming at: the student "turned away" with disgust from the world of objects and released in himself the want of moral virtue. Damascius concludes his story thus: "To the young man the shame and the astonishment in the indecent presentation brought a spiritual transformation." The spiritual alteration consisted in mastering the virtue of self-control—sophrosyne; he began to conduct himself according to its precepts.

In another fragment of his biography of Hypatia, Damascius returns once more to the virtue on behalf of which Hypatia fought her battle with the infatuated youngster. Characterizing her virtues in terms of Aristotle's ethical theory, he writes that she achieved the first, the so-called ethical or practical level of moral virtues, and within its sphere she incarnated two virtues: *dikaiosyne* (justice) and sophrosyne.[64] Other authors voice opinions similar to those of Damascius about Hypatia's personal values and moral exigencies. Socrates Scholasticus—within the range of cardinal virtues—mentions only sophrosyne to describe her ethical merits and system of conduct toward the outside world. In his opinion, the respect she commanded and the impression she made on people were due to her mastery of sophrosyne *(dia hyperballousan sophrosynen).*[65] As mentioned earlier, he also refers to this virtue when describing her contacts with representatives of the state authorities. This is also the virtue praised in her by two later historians, Cassiodorus and Nicephorus Callistus.[66]

From what we read in Synesius it follows that other students were more sensitive to the meaning of moral virtues than Damascius' *prosphoitetes* (disciple). Soon after his studies with Hypatia, when he himself began to mold his character, Synesius became a stern judge of others' shortcomings. For instance, he sharply admonished and rebuked Herculianus for having become a slave to "mundane" feelings and desires (*Ep*. 140). He begged and exhorted him to exercise disdain for all things of the lowest order ("contempt for everything here below") to achieve the philosophical state of *apatheia*—complete liberation from emotions and affections. He even demanded that he be discontent with the cultivation of the canon of the four virtues at their first—lowest—(civic) and second (cathartic) levels, and lift himself to the third and fourth levels: the contemplative and the paradigmatic, that is, to those levels on which—according to Neoplatonic ethics—the original ethical proficiencies fuse with their transcendental forms: "I am speaking, not of that manliness which springs from the first and earthly quarternion of the virtues, but the proportionate manliness amongst the virtues of the third and fourth degrees. You will enter into full possession of this force, when you learn to wonder at nothing here below."[67]

We do not know whether these reflections flow from Synesius' Neoplatonic readings or from Hypatia's requirements of her students. They could not have been excessive, since by the example of her dear student Synesius it seems clear that his teacher did not demand complete renunciation of all sensual and material ties. Synesius was a married man, he had progeny, and he did not want to separate from his wife when he was called to the bishopric (*Ep*. 105). From Hypatia's teachings he knew, after all, that the virtues of sophrosyne could be acted upon equally well in the single as in the married state.

In truth, Hypatia set the highest requirements for the cleansing of the soul through the practice of moral virtue only for herself. Only her sophrosyne manifested itself in complete sexual continence, in her famous virtue of chastity which, to be sure, strengthened her reputation for holiness spread by her disciples. She remained a virgin to the end of her life, always behaved moderately, practiced asceticism in everyday life (for instance, by wearing the philosophic tribon), and observed restraint and decency in every situation.[68] She was motivated in this respect not just by concern about her own existence but above all by concern about her students, to whom she sought to demonstrate by example that the mystic achieves freedom by humbling himself to and fusing with god, and not by gratifying natural wants.

Besides teaching ontology and ethics, Hypatia lectured on mathematics and astronomy. Synesius recalls the lectures with the same admiration and respect he expresses for those on pure philosophy. In this circle mathematics was but another, very important, instrument for acquiring metaphysical cognition. Its truths directed the students to a higher epistemological sphere, prepared them for generalizations, opened their eyes to ideal reality. The subject was called "divine geometry," and its "holy" principles, we remember, were applied to the achievement of reciprocal friendly relationships (*Ep.* 93).

Of all mathematical sciences auxiliary to metaphysical knowledge, Hypatia regarded astronomy as the highest. In *Ad Paeonium de dono* Synesius preserves her view that "astronomy is itself a divine form of knowledge." Hypatia also encouraged Synesius to build an astrolabe, an instrument for observing and examining heavenly bodies. "The most revered teacher" knew that the study of astronomy would open her students' minds to that area beyond which there is only the space of mystical experiences: "I consider it a science that opens up the way to ineffable theology."[69] In this way the "sacred rites of philosophy" would be made accessible to those pursuing traditional wisdom as well as to those studying the principles of mathematics, geometry, and astronomy: "And it [astronomy] proceeds to its demonstrations clearly and distinctly, making use of arithmetic and geometry as helpers; disciplines which one can properly call a fixed measure of truth."

The esteem in which Hypatia held astronomy and mathematics is confirmed by her active, scientific interest in those subjects. No titles of her philosophical works are extant, but reports survive about her mathematical and astronomical writings. Their titles allow us to reconstruct the topics of her lectures.[70] She presented the principles of geometry on the basis of Apollonius of Perge and Euclid, in whom her father was highly interested. For her lectures in arithmetic she availed herself of the handbook of Diophantus of Alexandria, the eminent algebraist of the early empire. Next to him she turned to Ptolemy as the indispensable authority for the explanation of mathematical truths. She also relied on Ptolemy in her course on astronomy. Numerous indications show that Ptolemy was exceptionally revered in Theon's home, which housed commentaries on his works written by both father and daughter, as well as the poetic eulogies honoring Ptolemy included in Synesius' *De dono* and preserved under Theon's name.

References in Synesius' letters to the Pythagorean mystique of numbers and to the philosophical and political concepts of the school indicate that Hypatia also introduced her students to the arcana of Pythagorean mathematics. Indeed, the fashion for Pythagoras prevailed in all Late Platonic circles; like Plato, he was regarded as a kind of "holy man" and chief moral authority.[71]

There is ground for belief that after Hypatia's death, in some Alexandrian circles she was celebrated and remembered as a mathematician rather than as a philosopher, and that, given the preservation of the titles, her mathematical works enjoyed a measure of popularity among successive generations of students. In his report of Hypatia's life Damascius uses this fact to belittle her as a thinker and to imply that she was an ordinary scholar-specialist. But by contrasting her with his master, the philosopher Isidore, "as only a mathematician against a true philosopher," he does not harm her much, for Damascius reports that her mathematical achievements were highly appreciated at the beginning of the sixth century, when he was writing his biography of Isidore.[72] Damascius likewise confirms that those who transmitted Hypatia's mathematical accomplishments to successive generations also knew that mathematics and astronomy were for her simply steps leading to cognition, which remained for her the central problem connected with the philosophy of being. All other extant sources refer to her, above all, as *philosophos*.

The kind of philosophizing that Hypatia practiced with her students, reconstructed on the basis of Synesius' accounts, is confirmed in other sources, among which Socrates' and Damascius' offer the most concrete evidence. Socrates writes: "She achieved such heights of erudition that she surpassed all the philosophers of her time, succeeded to the Platonic school derived from Plotinus, and delivered all the philosophy lectures to those who wished to listen." Socrates undoubtedly means that Hypatia's significance surpassed that of other Alexandrian philosophers of the end of the fourth and the beginning of the fifth centuries. In fact the other philosophers of that period mentioned in the sources seem to have sunk into obscurity.[73]

Socrates' much-disputed claim that Hypatia "succeeded to the Platonic school derived from Plotinus" probably means that she was conducting a small educational establishment of a closed philosophical circle, which in her day was common practice among renowned philosophers.[74] Clearly, she held no chair in philosophy financed by the city, nor was she a philosopher on the public payroll, as is sometimes asserted.[75] If a philosopher held this kind of position in Alexandria in the fourth and fifth centuries, the sources tend not to suppress the fact (see the cases of Hermeias and his son Ammonius) or to conceal membership in the Museion (see the case of Hypatia's father).

The view about Hypatia's public function as a teacher of philosophy in Alexandria is also confirmed in Damascius' work, where he writes: "Donning the philosopher's cloak [*tribon*] and making her way through the midst of the city she explained publicly [*exegeito demosia*] the writings of Plato or Aristotle, or any other philosopher." This enigmatic observation has provoked considerable controversy. First, it has been argued that *exegeito demosia* means that she held an official municipal appointment to the position of teacher of philosophy. Second, the expression has been used to call into question Hypatia's Platonism and to portray her as a roving people's philosopher, a kind of Cynic preacher.[76] Cameron, however, has proposed an original explanation for this disparaging characterization of her style and teaching: he sees in it Damascius' vindictive response to

Synesius' opinion of the Platonic Academy in Athens, at which Damascius was a master. In *Epistle* 136 Synesius observes: "Athens no longer has anything sublime except the country's famous names . . . Athens was formerly the dwelling-place of the wise: today the beekeepers alone bring it honor." Cameron thinks that Damascius took offense at these and other contemptuous remarks about the teachers of the Academy as well as those who practiced philosophy from a different perspective.[77]

It is hard to imagine a dignified woman philosopher of austere habits slouching through the streets of Alexandria talking to passersby eager to listen to a lecture on the history of philosophic systems. It appears that Damascius, notorious for his slovenly penmanship, crammed several pieces of information about Hypatia into one sentence. One of them refers to Hypatia's political activities and—connected with it—a certain type of public activity, another to her teaching. We shall return to the reference to her political activity in the next chapter; the reference to her teaching should be understood more strictly in relation to the claim that "she expounded publicly the works of Plato, Aristotle or other philosophers to whoever was eager to listen to her." This means that Hypatia was teaching publicly in the sense that—besides teaching a narrow circle of "initiates"—she also delivered lectures for a wider public. It does not mean at all that she was a street-corner preacher. The lectures were probably also delivered in her house, where she was regularly meeting with students of her esoteric circle. It is to these "public" lectures of Hypatia's that the anecdote mentioned earlier about the jealous bishop Cyril refers. Passing by Hypatia's house, he saw a large group of people gathered around it. They probably wanted to attend one of her lectures on the history of philosophy beginning with Plato and Aristotle. They also wanted to hear her comments on the works of famous mathematicians and astronomers. This type of lecture Hypatia may have also conducted outside her house, in various public lecture halls of the city.[78] On such occasions she left the house in a chariot—as both Socrates and Damascius tell us—and not on foot, as Damascius suggests elsewhere. These were the sort of lectures attended by state and city functionaries and people of various other occupations.

Hypatia's regular students, about whom Socrates writes so extravagantly, saying they came "from everywhere,"[79] visited her house daily. It was for these students, who were to occupy themselves with "divine matters only" (*Ep.* 154) throughout their lives, that Hypatia delivered lectures according to a secret schedule. In a circle whose members participated in the "philosophical mysteries," it was inadmissible "for the unclean to handle that which is pure" (*Ep.* 137). That Hypatia's most devoted disciples met with her often is also borne out by their mutual attachment. The kind of relations observable among Synesius, Olympius, and Herculianus are typical of those formed among young people in close association for several years. Hence the relationship with their teacher was a reflection of longlasting attachment and affection, and of constant devotion. They therefore referred to her not only as teacher of philosophy and benefactor, but also as mother and sister (*Ep.* 16). The feeling of attachment to their teacher was so deep that Synesius was ready to abandon his native land for her; he promised himself that he would remember his beloved Hypatia even in Hades (*Ep.* 124). Thus enraptured with their teacher's magnetic personality and with themselves, they believed god himself had brought them together (*Ep.* 137). They happened to meet in this exceptional spot on earth and at an exceptional time after the decline of Athens; in its place, "today Egypt has received and cherishes the fruitful wisdom of Hypatia" (*Ep.* 136). The inhabitants of Egypt and Alexandria may therefore partake in the fruits grown from the seeds of Hypatia's virtues and thought. For this reason, too, Synesius envies Herculianus his opportunity to extend his studies in Alexandria and to live in a place where "education flourishes among a multitude of men" (*Ep.* 130).

The initiates regard themselves not simply as fellow students but the happiest fellow students; after all, they belong to the "company of the blessed, the most holy and revered of the gods." Their attitude toward their teacher is reflected in the manner in which they address one another. As we have seen, their letters to one another are filled with expressions of affection; Synesius repeatedly assures his friends that he loves them (*Ep.* 143), and he uses expressions such as "dearest," a manner of speaking in common use at that time, expressing sympathy. After his departure from Alexandria Synesius ruefully observes that Herculianus most likely does not miss him; after all, he continues to associate with grand people: "there will be with you many like Synesius and many better than he" (*Ep.* 139).

Their community, which they liked best to call *hetairoi* (*Ep.* 137), was thus knitted together with deep ties. Indeed, it was anchored in immutable divine laws (*Epp.* 140, 143), which "demand that we who are united through the intellect, the best thing within us, should honour one another" (*Ep.* 137). Living in a community that constituted a microcosm reflecting the laws of the universe, they shared with Hypatia experiences that filled them with amazement. Hence in his letters to Herculianus Synesius repeatedly avows: "It was granted to you and me to experience marvelous things, the bare recital of which had seemed to be incredible" (*Ep.* 137).

For this reason, too, everything that Herculianus, Olympius, Synesius, Hesychius, and their close colleagues heard from their "common teacher" on the topic of the mysteries of philosophy, they kept in deep secret. In *Epistle* 137 Synesius even wonders whether he should entrust his philosophical reflections to letters to Herculianus, because they might fall into strangers' hands. And in *Epistle* 143 he admonishes and begs him to keep secret the holy dogmas that they have received together from Hypatia: "For my part I am, and I advise you also to be, a more careful guard over the mysteries of philosophy." To study together and preserve the knowledge received from Hypatia they formed on one occasion a union of four friends—not a singular practice in those times—corresponding to the Pythagorean *tetractys*.[80] Convinced that their association reflected the cosmic laws and interdependencies, they promised to themselves to preserve in secrecy all they saw at Hypatia's "with their own eyes" and heard "with their own ears." For it was obvious to them that the mysteries of being revealed by a genuine guide *(gnesia kathegemon)* should not fall among those who would trivialize and ultimately ridicule them. Quoting from Lysis the Pythagorean, Synesius wrote: "To explain philosophy to the mob is only to awaken among men a great contempt for things divine" *(Ep.* 143). This observation corresponds to their shared conviction that philosophy, if removed from the elite circles elected for its cultivation, would lose its true substance. Various charlatans and pseudophilosophers would abuse the knowledge about the divine reality to show off in front of simpletons, thus desecrating the inviolable truths. For the mob will never understand the mystery of god and the cosmos.[81]

Synesius retained these views throughout his life. Even after the change from a secular to a religious existence, philosophy remained for him a domain for the few; "I am far from sharing the views of the vulgar crowd on the subject . . . What can there be in common between the ordinary man and philosophy? Divine truth should remain hidden, but the vulgar need a different system" *(Ep.* 105). Only aristocrats, "the good and noble," members of the urban ruling classes of best descent, proud in their *eugeneia,* qualify for the "company of the blessed lady" *(Ep.* 139).

Their circle, of course, excludes women. Herculianus candidly admits to Synesius that he scorns women, even those truly devoted to him *(Ep.* 146; see also *Ep.* 132). After all, Hypatia, as a teacher of philosophy and an ethical master, transformed the concept of womanhood. Her moral mission, which found fulfillment in private activities as well as in spectacular public gestures, raised her high above her sex. She could say about herself what the Pythagorean Empedocles had said about himself, and Apollonius of Tyana later applied to himself: "Once I was both girl and boy."[82]

This proud Greek aristocrat (as Kingsley correctly characterizes her), though clad in the modest mantle of the philosopher, gathered around her a circle of young adepts living in a moral order circumscribed by philosophy, convinced that they were made of better clay than others. In this small group, as if taken straight out of the ideal Platonic state, the cult of aristocracy was intense. Synesius frequently stressed his Spartan lineage, as, surely, did his colleagues.

Although Hypatia taught the virtue of benevolence and appears to have praised Synesius' conduct as patron, calling him "a providence of other people" (*Ep.* 81),[83] the influential and well-connected young men in her circle extended their protective benevolence only to others of their class. The protégés of *Epistle* 81, Nicaeus and Philolaus, are presented to Hypatia as "two aristocratic young men." Thus, although Synesius proudly reiterates Hypatia's opinion of him—"All respect which was accorded to me by the mighty of this earth I employed solely to help others. The great were merely my instruments" (*Ep.* 81)— neither Hypatia nor her well-born friends would intervene with influential figures on behalf of individuals from lower strata of society.

Hypatia's disciples never lost their sense of superiority to other philosophers and other kinds of philosophizing. The circle's characteristic repudiation of lower social groups (*Ep.* 143) resurfaces in Synesius' *Dion, or about His Life,* written about 404. In it he sharply criticizes philosophers who wear white mantles but do not occupy themselves with philosophy seriously in line with the Greek literary tradition. They are "professional" proselytizers of wisdom, ordinary sophists circulating the divine truths of philosophy among the masses. The other group Synesius censures are people wearing black mantles—monks (*Ep.* 154; *Dion* 4–11).[84] Although in *Dion* Synesius shows interest in monastic life, he considers monks "barbarians," weaving-basket fanatics, wanting culture, loathing Hellenism.

Characteristically, Hypatia was the first to receive *Dion* for evaluation (*Ep.* 154). Sending her the work, Synesius reiterates the theses of his polemics with the "white" and "black" mantles, whom he incidentally calls his critics. Hypatia must have shared

Synesius' views; breathing air filled with the highest ideas of Hellenic *paideia,* they scorned monks because the latter rejected the Hellenic tradition. Thus it seems fairly certain that in Alexandria Hypatia's intellectual views and her circle's isolation were not universally well regarded.

The inadequacy of sources and the secretiveness of Hypatia's philosophic community have compelled scholars to speculate on the nature of the Neoplatonic philosophy practiced there. The question has been whether it was tied to the tradition of Plotinus and Porphyry or to that of Iamblichus. For Cameron, the characterization of philosophizing as "ineffable mysteries" proves that in this circle it was connected with some theurgic practices and thus had an Iamblichan character.[85] In Cameron's opinion Hypatia and her circle used the Chaldean Oracles, that "Bible" of Neoplatonism, including secret doctrines. What is more, he assumes that it was Antoninus, Sosipatra's son, who initiated Hypatia into the secrets of theurgy. After all, during Hypatia's youth Antoninus was teaching theurgic Platonism in Canopus, near Alexandria, where he settled after leaving Pergamon. He himself had been inducted into the secrets of theurgy by his mother.[86]

However, the sources do not mention that Hypatia had been trained in the discipline of theurgica, and they would surely convey such information if she had been so initiated. After all, they do so with regard to Sosipatra and Asclepigeneia—the daughter of Plutarch of Athens. The sources are quite specific in this respect: they also tell us that Asclepigeneia transmitted her knowledge to the philosopher Proclus, whose biographer Marinus records that Asclepigeneia divulged to Proclus the secret tradition and introduced him to theurgy.[87]

Words like *orgia, agoge,* and *anagoge,* known to have been used in Hypatia's circle to describe the process of philosophical theurgy, do not occur in accounts of Hypatia's teaching. The phrases and concepts used by Synesius indicate that he studied the biographies of eminent philosophers, including Porphyry and Iamblichus' *Life of Pythagorus,* Porphyry's *Life of Plotinus,*

Libanius' speeches, and Eunapius' *Lives of the Philosophers*. We encounter the same terms in Damascius' *Life of Isidore* and Marinus' *Life of Proclus*.[88] Clearly, the patterns of perfection and models of philosophical virtue presented in these works influenced Synesius' image of Hypatia. But it also seems likely that they were constitutive elements in Hypatia's own philosophizing. All the sources describe her, above all, as a Platonist. They mention that she taught Plato, Aristotle, and Plotinus, all of whom are associated with Neoplatonism. Since Damascius reports that besides these three systems, she was capable of presenting the views of other schools and philosophers, we may assume that diverse philosophical and theological texts were read in her circle.[89] In fact Hypatia and her students seem to have examined all writings that enhanced their sensitivity to things divine, that opened their eyes and minds to revelation. These works certainly included the Chaldean Oracles, since Synesius frequently refers to them in the *Hymns* and in other of his compositions, such as *On Dreams*.[90] These Hermetic texts, favored by Hypatia's father, were read and studied at their home, and Synesius' writings indicate that he, too, was familiar with them.[91] He also shows sympathy for the person and philosophy of the divine Hermes.[92] As Cameron's latest studies of *On Providence* demonstrate, Synesius' familiarity with the Egyptian-Greek religious, apocalyptic, demonologic literature originated in the period of studies with Hypatia and his encounter with Egyptian culture in Alexandria.[93]

Cameron correctly observes that "for all his enthusiasm for the Chaldean Oracles and his talk of 'ineffable mysteries' Synesius was essentially a cultural rather than a religious hellenist."[94] So indeed was Hypatia. Nowhere in the sources is she identified as a devout pagan, and her lectures, though described in mystical-religious terms, did not include theurgic ritualism so characteristic of groups cultivating the post-Iamblichan tradition of philosophy.[95] She made no endeavor to win the favor of or to master the numerous divine emanations—gods, demons, heroes. In her circle no magic methods were used to comprehend the nature of the world; there is no mention of sacrifices being offered to the gods, of cult objects being used, of night ceremonies, of statues being animated, or the like. Even John of Nikiu, although he portrays her as an ordinary witch practicing evil magic, says nothing about cult practices in connection with her.

Since Synesius likens Hypatia's lecturing to a religious ceremony, her classes must have had ingredients of ritual. In the close circle of her students she certainly did not confine herself to dry orations on philosophical truths and ideas. Synesius' letters reveal that her lectures were conducted in the form of dialogues on ethical and religious topics. Possibly, in order to achieve a state of awareness of the presence of god and spiritual perfection, they recited prayers and sang sacred hymns that exalted both their emotional and cognitive experience. For the same reason, they may also have read and recited texts with a Christian orientation. With Christians among her students, such a practice would be both understandable and desirable. Bizzochi is therefore right to assume that the genesis of Synesius' Christian hymns may be sought in the mystic meetings at Hypatia's home.[96] *Hymns* V and IX, which in Lacombrade's opinion, too, were composed during his studies with Hypatia, are imbued with the atmosphere of scholarship and sacredness that characterized their gatherings.[97] Even those composed somewhat later are infused with the spiritual aura of their sessions.[98]

In my view, a far more powerful reason for the secrecy of Hypatia's circle than its elitism was the depth of the experiences they shared. The singular state achieved through steadfast mental work and the cleansing of the soul through contemplation, immobility in rapture, and loss of contact with reality was indescribable: what was there to say about it except that one had experienced it? The "holy man" Apollonius alludes to the experience in *On Sacrifices* where he states that god was worshiped through silent ecstasy and through demonstrating one's own perfection.[99] Indeed, Synesius' *Hymns* are devoted to these experiences; he celebrates the blissful silence of the spheres over which God reigns. He also sought the secret tranquillity of contemplation during his priestly ministrations, which he viewed as "in-effable mysteries."

The evidence assembled on Hypatia's teaching and the circle of her students brings us closer to the philosophical milieu of Alexandria at the turn of the fourth and fifth centuries, the Late Platonic communities of master and disciples typical of late Hellenism.[100]

⌐ ·III·⌐

THE LIFE
AND DEATH
OF HYPATIA

Theon's Daughter and the Alexandrians

Hypatia spent her life in Alexandria. There is no evidence that she ever left the city—not even for a short time, to take up studies in Athens, as some scholars have suggested.[1] Alexandria was universally admired. It was the third largest city in the empire, the residence of the *praefectus Augustialis* (prefect of Egypt), the *dux Aegypti* (military commander of Egypt), and other imperial as well as city officials, and the seat of the Egyptian and Libyan churches.[2] It was a closed universe, fully shaped, finished, and framed, completely gratifying her spiritual needs. The Museion, the library, the waning pagan temples, the churches, the circles of theologians, philosophers, and rhetors, the mathematical and medical schools, a catechetical school and a rabbinical schul—all made up its framework and answered the intellectual and cultural wants of its inhabitants.

Here she lived with her father, Theon; here she gathered her students, who came from Alexandria, from other parts of Egypt, and from distant lands. She knew the vital problems of the city of which she was an esteemed resident. She moved in it freely in her chariot, showed herself in her characteristic tribon, called on influential officials, visited public and scientific institutions. A fixture of the city, as a scholar, a beautiful woman in her youth, a sovereign in her own right in the city, and witness to many of its events, she commanded respect and, in some circles, provoked controversy. Here, too, she would also become the object of anger, aggression, and degradation.[3]

In the sources the name of the Alexandrian Hypatia appears in two spellings, Hypatia and Hypateia, the former more often than the latter: it is the feminine form of Hypatios.[4] Hypatia was by no means a rare Hellenic name; it was used in pagan as well as in Christian families.[5] But as Nicephorus Gregoras, a Byzantine historian of the fourteenth century, reports, only the name of our woman philosopher eventually became synonymous with a wise and sagacious woman. It was he who called Eudocia, the wife of the emperor Constantine the Despot, son of Andronicus II Paleologus, a "second" Hypatia when describing her virtues, depth of education, and conversational skills.[6] His account suggests that in late Byzantine times women known for their love of the sciences and philosophy were proverbially referred to by this appellation.

In acknowledgment of Hypatia's intellectual attributes, after her death Michael Psellus bestowed on her the sobriquet "the Egyptian wise woman." Calling the roll of prominent women who applied themselves to literary and philosophical pursuits, he pointed to the Sybil, Sappho, Theano, and "the Egyptian woman philosopher."[7] He did not even have to mention her name, since every reader would know the person he had in mind.

Although we have no difficulties in determining Hypatia's city of birth, we face considerable obstacles in establishing her date of birth. It is widely thought that she was born around 370.[8] This dating rests on Hesychius' communication in *Suda* that the height of Hypatia's career came during the reign of the emperor Arcadius.[9] Birth in 370 would bring her to maturity in the year 400, in one sense the midpoint of the emperor's rule. But this date is neither certain nor satisfactory. Several indications from other sources prompt us to date her birth earlier.

John Malalas argues persuasively that at the time of her ghastly death Hypatia was an elderly woman[10]—not twenty-five years old (as Kingsley wants), nor even forty-five, as popularly assumed. Following Malalas, some scholars, including Wolf, correctly argue that Hypatia was born around 355 and was about sixty when she died.[11] Another interpretation of Hesychius' text might confirm Malalas' assertion. Its justification may be found in Penella's hypotheses about Hypatia's date of birth.[12] He points out that Arcadius was proclaimed Augustus in 383; consequently, his rule should be counted from that year and not from 395, the year his father, Theodosius I, died.

The biography of Synesius, Hypatia's favorite student, offers an additional argument in favor of the earlier date. Although the year of his birth, 370, is also a matter of conjecture, the period of his studies with Hypatia—the 390s—is a certainty.[13] Cameron likewise thinks that Synesius' year of birth falls somewhere from 368 to 370.[14] There can be no doubt that Synesius would have studied not with someone his own age but with a person his senior. The respectful manner in which he addresses his teacher does not accord with the picture of a twenty-year-old girl. It is hard to believe that at such an age she could have distinguished herself as singularly erudite in mathematics, astronomy, and philosophy.

According to *Suda* Hypatia's father, Theon, reached maturity during the reign of Theodosius I (379–395).[15] Malalas, however, maintains that his prime occurred in the time of Gratian, that is, between 367 and 383.[16] The early 360s seem more likely, since we know that in 364 Theon predicted eclipses of the sun and the moon, which he observed in Alexandria.[17] Such predictions would not have been recorded had they not issued from a mature scholar. Consequently, Hypatia's father must have been born around 335.[18]

The chronology of Theon's life is further obscured in *Suda,* where the astronomer and mathematician Pappus appears as Theon's contemporary.[19] The error rests on the premise that both mathematicians published Euclid's *Elements* and commented on Ptolemy's *Almagest,* whereas in fact Pappus did so around 320, and Theon in the 360s and 370s.[20] Although we are ignorant of the date of Theon's death, we are certain that he did not live long enough to witness his daughter's death. It is my assumption that he died sometime in the first years of the fifth century.

Theon was a highly educated scholar, a mathematician and astronomer. Thanks to *Suda,* we know that he was a member of the Alexandrian Museion *(ho ek tou Mouseiou),* and the epithets *Aigyptios* and *Alexandreus* point to his Greek-Egyptian heritage and connections with and devotion to his native city and the multilingual Alexandrian tradition.[21]

Indeed, Theon, like his daughter, did not leave Alexandria; he nurtured himself on the spiritual wealth of this intellectually affluent city. He devoted his scholarship to the study of his eminent predecessors Euclid and Ptolemy; he was undoubtedly interested in philosophy, but more so in pagan religious literature and old Greek practices of divination. Unlike his daughter, he did not teach philosophy. Neoplatonic philosophy was only one ingredient of his education, but as a scholar-mathematician he is called a philosopher by Socrates Scholasticus, Hesychius, and Theophanes;[22] Malalas even refers to him as "the wisest philosopher."[23] In the entry on Theon in *Suda,* both Theon and Pappus are called philosophers. Because of his astronomical knowledge and studies of magic, astrological sources refer to him as "sage" and "philosopher."[24]

Several of Theon's mathematical and astronomical works have survived: Euclid's *Elements,* designed for students; *The Data;* and *The Optics.*[25] Known to and copied by Byzantines, they were used for modern editions of Euclid's texts.[26] Theon was also a superior commentator on Ptolemy's mathematical and astronomical works. He wrote commentaries on the thirteen books of *Almagest (Syntaxsis mathematica)* following the tracks— and in many fragments using the text—of his compatriot Pappus.[27] Theon also wrote two commentaries on Ptolemy's *Handy Tables: The Great Commentary,* in five books; and *The Little Commentary,* in one.[28]

Theon did not work alone; he had associates. It is likely that

Pappus, his senior, occasionally kept him company, since Theon made use of his commentaries on *Almagest*. Two other associates were mathematicians known only by their first names, Eulalius and Origenes, to whom he dedicated *The Great Commentary* on the *Handy Tables* of Ptolemy; they may also have been students of Theon's, since he refers to them as *hetairoi,* companions.[29] To another student, Epiphanius, he dedicated *The Little Commentary,* the fourth book of *The Great Commentary,* and an apostrophe in the introduction to the commentary on *Almagest.*[30] In these works Epiphanius is called *teknon,* child (in the dedication, *teknon Epiphanie*). These dedications have led some scholars to infer that he was Hypatia's brother.[31] But in late Hellenic scientific circles as well as in Hermetic and Gnostic communities, masters commonly addressed their students in this manner.[32] When Theon mentions his daughter as an associate, he calls her *thygater.*[33]

Among Theon's scientific associates, Hypatia was his closest collaborator. Given the evidence of Theon's dedications, his other students appear to have applied themselves assiduously to science, and especially to Ptolemy's works; but only the titles of Hypatia's mathematical studies are extant. As her father's child and associate, she is highly esteemed in the sources, which describe her as a mathematician who surpassed her father's talents. Philostorgius, for example, writes that having been introduced by her father to the arcana of mathematics, she eclipsed her teacher not only in mathematics but, above all, in astronomy. Hesychius, recalling Hypatia's sagacity and fame, stresses her own abilities in the context of her work with her father. Damascius in turn, as if summarizing his predecessors' opinions, remarks that she was "by nature more refined and talented than her father." As we remember, in another fragment Damascius disparages Hypatia's philosophical skills and presents her—in contrast to the philosopher Isidore—only as a mathematician. Finally, at the turn of the thirteenth and fourteenth centuries, Nicephorus Callistus recalls the excellent education Hypatia received from her father, which she developed and cultivated.

Although the sources praise Hypatia's mathematical talent, historians of mathematics have treated Theon better than his daughter.[34] The incongruity reflects Hypatia's greater versatility as a scholar interested not just in mathematics but in "all philosophy." In addition, beginning with Socrates and Philostorgius, historians writing about her achievements as a mathematician have praised her accomplishments as a humanist. Moreover, Theon's mathematical fame has been fostered by the survival of his editions of Greek mathematicians' writings, whereas we have not had Hypatia's works (although this, as we shall see, is beginning to change).

Hesychius' list of Hypatia's mathematical titles suggests that she occupied herself with the works of native Alexandrian mathematicians; she wrote commentaries on Apollonius of Perge, who lived in the third century B.C.; on Diophantus, who lived around the middle of the third century A.D.; and on a piece titled *The Astronomical Canon.*[35] Apollonius' work, *The Conic Sections,* was in geometry; Perl has attempted to reconstruct Hypatia's commentary on it.[36] Diophantus was and continues to be considered the most difficult mathematician of antiquity. Several scholars believe that the survival of the bulk of his *Arithmetica* is due to the quality of Hypatia's elucidations.[37] Out of thirteen books of the original we have six in Greek and four translated into Arabic in the ninth century. They contain notes, remarks, and interpolations that may come from Hypatia's commentary. If this is the case, the nature and content of her commentaries on the Alexandrian mathematicians were exegetical, intended for students.[38]

If some of Hypatia's commentary on Diophantus could survive, then another thesis of Cameron's seems even more likely to be valid. It deals with the question of Hypatia's commentary on the writings of Ptolemy. Until recently scholars thought that Hypatia revised Theon's commentary on *Almagest.* The view was based on the title of the commentary on the third book of *Almagest,* which read as follows: "Commentary by Theon of Alexandria on Book III of Ptolemy's *Almagest,* edition revised by my daughter Hypatia, the philosopher."[39] Cameron, who has analyzed Theon's titles for other books of *Almagest* and for other scholarly texts of late antiquity, concludes that Hypatia corrected not her father's commentary but the text of *Almagest* itself. Thus, the extant text of *Almagest* could have been prepared, at least partly, by Hypatia.[40]

Moreover, Hypatia may have also prepared a new edition of Ptolemy's *Handy Tables,* which in Hesychius appears under the title *The Astronomical Canon.* She was probably busy with it when Theon was writing both commentaries (the "large" and the "small") to Ptolemy's work.[41] Therefore, Cameron's observation that there is no reason to lament the complete loss of Hypatia's writings seems justified. The extant texts of Ptolemy's *Almagest* and *Handy Tables* were probably prepared for publication by Hypatia.

Hypatia's opinion about astronomy as a venerable science and Philostorgius' claim that her astronomical competence exceeded her father's lend credence to Cameron's concrete arguments.[42] There is a possibility that scholars like Cameron, Toomer, and Knorr, working on the texts of Greek mathematicians, will in time effect a change in the views on the question of Hypatia's intellectual legacy. It may be already taken for granted that Hypatia will be admitted into the history of mathematics and astronomy as a scholar known not only by the titles of her works but also by their contents.

As long as Theon was alive, he worked on his mathematical predecessors with a group of close associates under his guidance. After his death Hypatia appears to have continued the project independently, as a mature scholar in her own right. Those of her students whose names we know do not seem to have operated as her associates; our sources, and especially Synesius' letters, indicate that she lectured to them on mathematical and astronomical matters but did not involve them in editing or commenting on the texts of Alexandrian mathematicians and astronomers.

Instead, we learn that Hypatia initiated her students (as did, perhaps, her father) into the more practical business of studying the mathematical-astronomical secret mysteries. We may recall here that as a result of her teaching Synesius was able to construct an astrolabe (*De dono* 4). For this purpose, of course, he had to be familiar with the principles of geometry that he mastered attending her lectures on the theory of Apollonius of Perge. The instrument, which measures the position of stars and planets, is called *organon* in *De dono* (5). It was intended as a gift for his friend Paeonius, a high-ranking state official in Constantinople.

There is no doubt that Hypatia learned the construction of the planisphere from her father. Consequently, both may have advised Synesius on the project. For we know that Theon wrote a treatise on the construction of such an instrument; *Suda* tells us it was titled *On the Small Astrolabe*.[43] The original version of the treatise has not survived, but its content has been restored on the basis of the works of later authors, beginning with Arab writers of the seventh century.[44] In his *Address to Paeonius (Ad Paeonium de dono)* Synesius does not mention Theon's little treatise; he alludes to Ptolemy as his predecessor in the construction of the astrolabe. Hence Neugebauer convincingly suggests that Synesius sent his gift and the enclosed letter describing the *organon* before Theon wrote *On the Small Astrolabe*.[45] The vague, indeed opaque, description of the appearance and operation of the device is additional proof that Synesius was ignorant of Theon's exposition, which we know from later quotations was lucid.

Neugebauer's hypothesis that Theon was still living when Synesius experimented with astronomical instruments permits us to speculate further on the date of Theon's death. The letter to Paeonius was written, and the gift presented, during Synesius' mission to Constantinople (although a copy of the letter was sent to Hypatia only in 404; *Ep.* 154). It is therefore possible that Theon was still alive during Synesius' mission and only then writing his treatise. He may then have died, as I suggested earlier, in the first years of the fifth century.[46]

We have already called attention to the differences in the intellectual interests of father and daughter. Theon was not attracted to theoretical philosophy. But he too had nonscientific tastes. Like Hypatia, he loved "Hellenism," although his affection for things Greek was, above all, religious in nature. Endowed with a literary talent, he expressed his devotion in poetic form. Malalas observes: "The most learned scholar and philosopher taught and interpreted astronomical writings and wrote commentaries on the books of Hermes Trismegistus and Orpheus."[47]

We thus learn that Theon not only commented on and wrote purely scientific works but also explicated treatises (most likely astrological ones) and the Orphics' texts—probably their hymns, which were highly admired by the Neoplatonists. In *Suda* we find titles or descriptions of other short writings of Theon's that confirm Malalas' statements about his interests in pagan religious practices and the movements of heavenly bodies: *On Signs and the Examination of Birds and the Croaking of Ravens,* and two essays on the function of the star Syrius and the influence of planetary spheres on the Nile.[48]

From this meager information we may at least tentatively conclude that Hypatia's father, apart from working on specific scientific projects, was also studying the secrets of the physical world and investigating the truths revealed by Hermes and Orpheus. The titles of these esoteric little pieces show a man attracted to numbers as well as to the voices of nature. For him reality was filled with signs from the planets and living creatures. The "magic of the world" impressed him more than the philosophers' arguments. His way of seeing and studying reality was different from that of his daughter. The interpretation of omens attracted him more than philosophical inquiry. The mysterious "adhesive" of the world was more accessible to him in astrological prophesies, in the cry of the birds proclaiming god's will, and in Hermes' revelation than in the thoughts of Plato and Aristotle.

Consequently, we should not be surprised to discover Theon as the author of poems on astrological themes included in the collections of the *Greek Anthology*. There are two poems, one of which appears now in *Corpus Hermeticum,* ascribed to Hermes himself.[49] In older editions of the *Greek Anthology* this poem figures under the name of either Theon or Hermes.[50] Titled *Peri heimarmenes,* it contains a monostich supposedly composed by Theon.[51] The poem enumerates in the "cosmic chaos" the sparkling bodies of the seven spheres of the universe: Jove, Mars, Venus, the Moon, Saturn, the Sun, Mercury. They embed the germs of the inflexible resolutions of Destiny *(moira).* The internal intelligence and power of the stars determine our condition from birth on. They predispose our psychic states and temperaments. This astronomical determinism, says Hermes/Theon, cannot be overcome, and the operation of particular planets is strictly circumscribed (for instance, Mars gives to people a violent and angry temperament). The powers of Destiny, the planetary spheres, are sustained by the lord of the immutable laws of the universe, the god of eternal time—Aion.[52]

The other poem, ascribed exclusively to Theon, manifests even more explicitly his devotion to the starry skies, the perfect world of the gods beyond the sphere of the moon. Dedicated to Ptolemy, it eulogizes the creator of the new model of the universe. Thus it seems that this commentator on Ptolemy's erudition and discoveries wrote a poem in praise of his talents.[53] The poem portrays Ptolemy as the gods' elect. His genius carried him high and transported him to the region of heavenly creatures, for his mind penetrated the laws governing the planetary spheres, and he beheld the immutable principles of Destiny ruling the cosmos. Destiny's reason belongs to the world of "ether" and not to the polluted world of earthly matter.

Both of these poems elaborate upon the distinction between "heaven" and "nature," between the sphere filled with ether and the reality of earthly existence. Yet splinters of a higher, divine substance reside in our hearts and minds; they can be activated and enhanced through effort and will. That is what Ptolemy achieved: through superhuman effort he tore himself away from the mundane region of "dismal muddiness" (as

Theon says in the language of the Orphics)[54] and was accorded the luminous perfection of divine beings.

Two other poems preserved under the name Theon differ from these in both tone and substance.[55] They contain no raptures over cosmic space, no planetolatria; rather, they are epigrams in the classic style suggestive of the epigrams of the lyric poets Archilochus and Mimnermus. Both include reminiscences of the sea. One tells about a mother's despair over the death of her son, a young sailor. His "grave" is the abysmal, cold sea, which swallowed up his body; the only commemoration of him is the circling of sea birds over the place of his "burial." In the other epigram, the poet animates and anthropomorphizes a shield, which turns itself into a faithful and dedicated servant to its master. During a dire sea battle it saves his life by carrying him from the wrecked ship to a safe haven, while all the other sailors perish.

For his poetry Theon earned no special praise from fellow poets. They admired him only for his mathematical achievements and for his passion for astronomy. Thus, Pallas recollected with reverence his erudition;[56] Leon the Philosopher (around 900) considered Theon an adornment to Alexandria and—next to Proclus—the wisest of men: one (Theon) measured the skies and penetrated their secrets; the other (Proclus) calculated the size of the earth.[57] And as an authority on astrological secrets Theon was celebrated by authors of magic-astrological pseudo-epigraphs. A casual look at the indexes of some volumes of the *Catalogus Codicum Astrologorum Graecorum* reveals that the name of Theon the Alexandrian appears in numerous works of that type, composed in various periods.[58]

For scholars of Alexandria of late antiquity, such as G. Fowden and J. C. Haas, Theon's tastes are unexceptional.[59] Virtually all Alexandrian mathematicians were interested in the occult sciences. Theon's down-to-earth knowledge went hand in hand with interests in divination, astrology, and Hermeticism. In this milieu, it was rather his daughter, with her more rational attitude toward the world and the Hellenic tradition, who raised her compatriots' eyebrows. For Alexandria in the fourth century was notorious for its fortune-tellers; after all, astrology was taught in its schools. Sundry astrologers operated in the city; the names of some of them have survived to our day. To the best of our knowledge, they were simultaneously regarded as mathematicians. Among them was Paulus of Alexandria, noted for his handbook on astronomy and astrology.[60] There was also an anonymous expert on the mysteries of the skies, named "the astrologer of the year 379," whose work is unknown by title but three chapters of which are extant; they deal with the origin and the principles of astrology.[61] Yet another was Hephaistion of Thebes, the last representative of fourth-century astrology; extracts from his astronomical handbook were titled *Apotelesmatica* or *Astronomica*.[62] These astronomers may have been acquaintances of Theon and the young Hypatia.

Thus we have some notion of the atmosphere in which Hypatia grew up, and of the pursuits—besides philosophical studies—to which her students were drawn. Our assumptions (discussed in Chapter II) about the literature read in their circle have recently been substantiated by analyses of the sources treating Theon. Steeped in tradition, the family was surely reading Hermes' revelation, the Orphics' theological writings, texts on Greek divination, handbooks on astrology.

These subjects left a mark on Synesius' writings. After returning home from another visit in Alexandria around 405, "inspired by god himself" he composed a treatise overnight and sent it immediately to Hypatia for criticism (*Ep.* 154). This work, titled *On Dreams,* deals with prediction of the future through the interpretation of dreams as refined by Neoplatonic philosophy. It expresses great appreciation for the capacity of the human soul for divination: "The superiority of God over man, and man over beast, is due to knowledge—a gift which the Deity possesses by nature, but which man can gain, to any full extent, only through divination."[63]

The same dispatch to Hypatia included another work, the treatise *Dion,* reflecting the influence of Hermetic writings read at Theon's home. In it Synesius lists the most saintly and the wisest men in history: Amous (Ammon), Zoroaster, Antony, and Hermes.[64] He also refers to Hermes' wisdom in *On Kingship, On Providence,* and other writings (such as the *Hymns*).[65]

To the end of his life Synesius sustained his interest, developed in Alexandria, in astronomy, the construction of scientific instruments, and the literature of the occult and religion, including prediction of the future. In 413, the year of his death, he sent four letters to Hypatia (*Epp.* 10, 15, 16, and 81). They are filled with sorrow and resignation, reflecting both the great burdens of his office and grief at the death of all his children, three sons. He feels lonely and deserted, and he complains about the absence of letters from the beloved teacher; he craves her words of consolation. In *Epistle* 15 he asks Hypatia to "forge" for him an instrument called a hydroscope, used for measuring the weight of liquids.[66] He describes what the instrument should look like and asserts that it will give him joy and uplift his heart: "I am in such evil fortune that I need a hydroscope." The words are intriguing. It is difficult to understand why a man oppressed by personal, ecclesiastical, and political adversity, desolate and lonely, would need a hydrometric instrument designed for chemical experiments.

The hydroscope, however, was probably used for more than strictly scientific purposes. In contrast to Lacombrade, I believe that Synesius wanted to use the instrument for divination.[67] A contemporary source provides confirmation: in an astrological work Hephaistion of Thebes states that the hydroscope, like the astrolabe, may be utilized in astrology, for the preparation of horoscopes, for the divination of future events. Synesius, crushed by despair, forsaken by his closest kin, was seeking consolation and deliverance in hydromancy. He wanted to consult with the gods of water about his future.[68] To save himself, to deliver his soul, he needed to hear the voice of Destiny, to decipher the will of the gods concerning his future, hoping it would be better than the present.

Synesius' action was not unusual; in this period people commonly resorted to hydroscopic instruments and other means of divining the future. And Synesius' study of the physical sciences and occult literature had begun in his youth, at least as early as his studies with Hypatia. His request to her was, therefore, not a momentary impulse, but a reflection of a long-standing activity rooted in his Alexandrian days. It is not surprising that this disciple of Hypatia (and perhaps of Theon), engrossed in dream interpretation, astrology, and physical experiments, came to be recognized as one of the earliest adepts in the secrets of alchemy.[69]

While Hypatia's students were examining philosophical questions, studying mathematical sciences, reading diverse religious literature, and conducting astronomical experiments, momentous events were taking place in Alexandria in connection with the patriarch Theophilus' activities. From the beginning of his pontificate, in 385, he had conducted a campaign against paganism in the city, expunging through various methods the religious cults still in existence.[70] With the outbreak of riots sparked by the church's appropriation of pagan temples, Theophilus seized the opportunity to strike a blow at the Serapeum, once the cult center in Alexandria.[71] The action against the shrine took place in either 391 or 392.[72] It must have occurred however, after the emperor Theodosius I's edict of June 391, which, by prohibiting cult practices, opened the way for the destruction of pagan cult places.[73]

A body of Alexandrian pagans, whose numbers were still substantial,[74] barricaded themselves in the temple, making sallies on the besieging Christians. This gave Theophilus a pretext to turn to the civil and military authorities for help. The matter was terminated by an edict from the emperor ordering the pagans to leave the temple, proclaiming the killed Christians martyrs, and handing the Serapeum over to the church. The magnificent statue of the god Serapis, the work of Bryaxis, was shattered into pieces by a soldier's ax.[75]

The historical sources state that Alexandrian luminaries assisted the pagans in their defense of the holy objects and cult symbols. One of them, the Neoplatonic philosopher Olympius, assumed leadership in the resistance in the Serapeum; the pagans were joined by Ammonius and Helladius, teachers of Greek language and literature; and by the poet Palladas and probably by the poet Claudian.

Even earlier, another Neoplatonic philosopher, Antoninus, Sosipatra's son and a disciple of Aedesius (a student of Iamblichus), had foretold the fall and ruin of the Serapeum. Although he did not live to see his prophecy fulfilled, for much of his life he was overcome with fear and anxiety about the future of religion and culture once the old gods were removed and their chief cult center in Alexandria ruined.

Given the support of the Alexandrian intellectual elite for the defenders of the old faith, the question inevitably arises how Hypatia stood on the issue. After all, in the early 390s she was already a famed and esteemed philosopher. Why did she not join Olympius in defending the threatened sacred objects of the Serapeum? Why did she not, along with her students, give moral aid to the defenders? We can understand her silence by looking more closely at the traits of the philosophers mentioned above.

Antoninus, who died before these events, was strongly tied to the cult of Serapis through his prophetic and religious activity. Hypatia's junior—he was born around 320—he moved from Pergamon to the Canopus district, near Alexandria at the mouth of the Nile. He died shortly before the destruction of the temples of the god Serapis in Alexandria and in Canopus (also ordered by Theophilus).[76]

In Canopus—probably in a temple district—Antoninus gathered students and taught them Platonic philosophy, which he combined with religious practices and secret ceremonies. He led a profoundly ascetic life, which included abstinence, and was devoted to the contemplation of divine creation. From his mother he inherited the gift of clairvoyance. All these attributes rendered him "divine," although he looked like an ordinary mortal and did not shun human company. His spiritual singularity, his internal radiance, attracted young men and old to Canopus by all available means of transportation. As a result the temple there was always crowded to capacity, with young people performing sacerdotal duties. Although Eunapius claims that Antoninus did not demonstrate any inclinations toward theurgic practices "because he kept a wary eye on the imperial views and policy, which were opposed to these practices,"[77] we know that Antoninus was a typical practitioner of Neoplatonic theurgy. As a philosopher-priest he remained in direct contact with the gods. If someone turned to him with a question about things divine, he silently raised his eyes toward heaven as if looking for an answer there. But he responded to questions connected with philosophy and Platonic logic. Exercising his religious and prophetic gift, Antoninus foretold the fall of the cult of the old gods and the destruction of the temples in Alexandria and Canopus. He recognized the implications of the legislation under Theodosius I, he saw through the schemes of the bishops seated on the throne of St. Mark, and he trembled with anxiety about the future of the old cultural values.[78]

The philosopher who actively participated in the defense of the Serapeum was the Neoplatonist Olympius. Church historians (Rufinus, Sozomenos) and Damascius in his *Life of Isidore* relate how, clad in the philosophical mantle, he placed himself at the head of the defenders.[79] He affirmed the sense of their struggle so powerfully that nobody could resist the words that "flowed out of his holy mouth" as he called for total sacrifice in defense of the sacred symbols of their ancestors' religion.[80] Like Antoninus, Olympius seemed an immortal being, and the deed accomplished through him of divine rather than human measure. When the defenders' morale flagged as they watched the destruction of the statues of the gods, he repeatedly assured them that the spirit dwelling in the statues departed to heaven; only their earthly manifestation was destroyed. Under his leadership the pagans made forays among the Christians, capturing, torturing, and crucifying them. Among those killed was the renowned rhetor Gessius.

Even before the outbreak of the conflict in 391/392, Olympius was known among Alexandrians as a servant and faithful confessor of Serapis. Tall, handsome, well-proportioned, and attractive, he had come from his native Cilicia to Alexandria to serve the god.[81] He was a master of all the cult rites, and he taught people how to conduct traditional ceremonies. Recalling the old creeds, he demonstrated their beauty and asserted that serving the gods brought bliss. He frequently admonished his listeners to safeguard the ancestral faith as their most precious treasure. Accordingly, the young and the old called him *hierodidaskalos;* Olympius' spirituality, moral authority, knowledge of the gods, and appearance led people to believe that this public teacher of religion was filled with god *(pleres tou theou).* Like Antoninus, he was endowed with the gift of prophesying on the future of the pagan religion. He too predicted to his disciples the fall of the temple of Serapis. When it came to pass, Damascius concluded that Olympius' visionary disposition was indeed deeply connected with the divine powers ruling the world.[82]

We know far less about the two Alexandrian grammarians who participated in the defense of the Serapeum, and what scraps of information we have come from Socrates Scholasticus.[83] Ammonius was a priest of Thoth (Hermes) and Helladius–Ammon (Zeus). In Constantinople, where they fled after the unrest of 391/392, both looked back on the events in Alexandria with pain and lamented the defeat dealt to Hellenic religion. Ammonius in particular despaired over the destruction of the statues of the gods and the ridicule to which they were subjected; on Theophilus' order the statute of the god Thoth (with the head of a baboon) had been exhibited to the mob, who had mocked its sacredness. Helladius, for his part, took pride in having killed nine Christians in the street skirmishes.

After the fall of the Serapeum, Ammonius, Helladius, Claudian, and other unnamed pagans left Alexandria, as did Olympius. When the emperor's edict ordering the destruction of the temple was proclaimed and soldiers and Christians began their occupation of the Serapeum, he escaped to Italy by sea and was not heard of again.[84] Claudian eventually settled in Rome, where he devoted himself to creative and political activity.[85] Palladas remained in Alexandria but was deprived of the salary allotted him by the city for teaching Greek literature.[86]

Hypatia's philosophical activity was not constrained, and her students did not have to look for a new teacher. She was not seen at any sites of the battles between pagans and Christians. Despite apparent affinities with Antoninus and Olympius, suggested by their common philosophical language, she felt no attraction to Greek polytheism or the local cults. For her, pagan beliefs were only beautiful embellishments to the spiritual Hellenic tradition that she so valued and cultivated. She felt no compulsion to support her Platonism with theurgy and ritual practices, divination, or magic; neither did service to a god with the head of a baboon have a place in the transcendentalism she professed. Moreover, philosophers like Antoninus and Olympius were not of her "company"; they did not fit into her spiritual environment. In her opinion, Olympius was probably a typical *demodidaskolos,* a public teacher of wisdom preaching the truths of "holy philosophy" to the lower classes. The aristocratic lady of Alexandrian philosophy did not direct her teachings to such audiences; she did not seek to stimulate love of god in them. To judge from the silence of the sources, she found no satisfaction in popular polytheism and did not participate in pagan cult practices. Her students came from the social elite; they were wealthy and influential. Furthermore, their circle included sympathizers with Christianity. Hypatia could not boast of having killed Christians. She and her students could not have been at the Serapeum.

The Circumstances of Hypatia's Death

It was under such social and religious circumstances, in a scientific environment created by her father, in a circle of students engaged in sophisticated philosophic discourse, that Hypatia's life was spent, until October 15, 412, the day Theophilus died. Referred to frequently as the "church's pharaoh," like his successor Cyril his harsh and authoritarian conduct provoked resentment among Alexandrian pagans and also complaints from monks of the desert Nitria (some of them, the so-called Origenists, left Egypt); from the bishop of Constantinople, John Chrysostom, whom he harassed; and from various ecclesiastical groups in the East.[87]

But Hypatia and her circle had no reason to complain about Bishop Theophilus. Those attending her Neoplatonic courses were not threatened with any persecution (which the philosopher Olympius so feared); they were able to pursue their studies. Hypatia herself, not needing to conceal her non-Christian religiosity, enjoyed full intellectual independence and the tolerance of the ecclesiastical authorities.

These circumstances began to change when Theophilus' nephew Cyril was elected to the bishopric of St. Mark's. It soon became clear that Hypatia would enjoy no accord with the patriarch. Church historians today express great respect for Cyril as a theologian and dogmatist,[88] but his contemporaries perceived him differently. The sources describe him as an impetuous, power-hungry man more relentless in pursuit of authority than his predecessor and uncle; he aroused strong opposition in Egypt.

Cyril's very election as Theophilus' successor caused unrest in Alexandria and provoked contention between two ecclesiastical parties. One party wanted Timothy, Theophilus' archdeacon, as successor to the bishopric; the other supported Cyril. Timothy's followers had the backing of the military chief commander Abundantius *(comes rei militaris per Aegyptum),* the representative of the imperial authority.[89] It is not clear whether he acted on instructions from the emperor. Rougé doubts it; he thinks Abundantius acted from personal motives.[90] Besides, Rougé believes he commanded only a detachment stationed in Alexandria. After three days of fighting Cyril, the victor in the contest, was installed as bishop, on October 17, 412.

Socrates, to whom we owe our knowledge about these events, remarks that Cyril's election brought a gradual but significant extension of episcopal authority to public, municipal affairs.[91] He began with a battle for the purity of the faith by moving against groups that did not hold orthodox beliefs. He expelled the Novatians from the city, closing their churches, confiscating their liturgical objects, and depriving their bishop of all rights.[92]

Next he turned against the Jews. Socrates relates that in his action against them, Cyril took advantage of events initiated by the Jews themselves.[93] Instead of celebrating the sabbath—says Socrates—and reading the Law, they attended the theater on Saturdays to watch dance performances, and they engaged in brawls with Christians. One Saturday, as the prefect Orestes was in the theater announcing an ordinance on pantomimic performances, a brawl broke out between believers of the two religions. During Orestes' speech the Jews cried out that there were agents of Cyril among the audience, agents who had come to sow disorder and to dog the activity of the emperor's envoy in the city. The prefect, who had just managed to bring calm and order to Alexandria, was upset by the disturbance and decided to listen to the Jewish spectators' grievances. Shouting, they demanded, above all, the dismissal of Hierax, an Alexandrian teacher and Cyril's sycophant. They accused him of being an informer and of fomenting disorder. Orestes, who already resented the bishop's appropriation of many prerogatives that had formerly belonged to the emperor's officials, ordered Hierax arrested and tortured.

The prefect's action provoked Cyril's anger; Hierax was indeed one of his confidants. Cyril summoned the leaders of the Jewish community and threatened them with serious consequences if they continued to taunt and antagonize Christians. This interview increased the Jews' rancor, and they began to carry out ambushes against Christians. One night some of them raised an alarm that the church of St. Alexander was on fire. When the Christians ran to save their church, the Jews attacked them, killing many. In response Cyril rushed with a large crowd to the Jewish district, surrounded the synagogue, permitted the plunder of Jewish property, and started chasing the Jews out of the city. Socrates claims that every one of the Jews, who had lived in Alexandria since Alexander the Great, was driven out. Although he surely exaggerated, undoubtedly a great many Jews did leave, and their expulsion must have adversely affected the city's economy.[94] Clearly, Cyril took advantage of the event to get rid of the greatest possible number of Jews, for doing so would weaken the traditional animosity between the confessions and reduce the number of adversaries against the policy of the church in Alexandria.[95]

Enraged by Cyril's measures, Orestes reported the incidents to the emperor; Cyril did likewise. Socrates remains silent on the emperor's reaction, saying only that Cyril attempted a reconciliation, sending a delegation to Orestes. Socrates stresses that a group of Alexandrians compelled Cyril to try to come to terms with Orestes. These people must have been members of the Christian community for Socrates uses the same term *(laos)* elsewhere to identify the people connected with the church. It is therefore obvious that some Christians wanted the patriarch to cooperate with the secular authorities. Cyril is said to have shown Orestes the New Testament, asking him to accept its truths and to exercise magnanimity. Orestes, however, refused to cooperate with the patriarch. Cyril felt powerless, and people from various religious groups associated with him began to contemplate other methods of applying pressure on the prefect.

Among the first to come openly to his aid (and surely with his encouragement) were 500 monks who left their hermetic lairs in Nitria and entered the city in force. Theophilus had already used them in fights against pagans as well as in doctrinal conflicts.[96] One day they confronted Orestes as he was riding through the city, insulted him, and accused him of paganism. The prefect's protestations that he was a Christian baptized by the bishop of Constantinople had no effect.[97] One of the monks—Ammonius—hit him in the head with a stone. The prefect began to bleed profusely, and his horror-stricken guard scattered, but a group of Alexandrians (probably Christians) rushed to his defense. Ammonius was caught and brought before Orestes while the crowd dispersed the monks. Orestes sentenced Ammonius to tortures that resulted in his death. The prefect then dispatched a report on the affair to the imperial chancellery. Cyril did likewise, characterizing the matter as a religious struggle and claiming Ammonius as a martyr. Socrates' text, however, makes it clear that moderate Christians, aware of the monk's crime, criticized Cyril on his stand. Yielding, the bishop stopped propagandizing the affair.

But the head of the church and the representative of imperial power remained at odds; of the two, Orestes was the more obdurate. The bloody conflict between the Christians and the Jews, the expulsion of the latter from the city, the monks' attempt on his life, and Cyril's other religious demonstrations fed his obstinacy. The question then arises, on what did this obstinacy rest? After all, he was a recent arrival in Alexandria, little known, and from the beginning of his tenure an object of attacks by the church and the groups associated with it.

Clearly, Orestes' unyielding position toward the patriarch's actions had strong backing from influential people, members of the ruling class in the city and its environs. One of the notables who supported him was Hypatia—a friend from the beginning of his term in office in Alexandria.

Hypatia's support of Orestes—a momentous move—is reported by Socrates in a short but significant sentence. He says that men "of the Christian population" started to spread a slanderous rumor that Hypatia was the lion in the path to a reconciliation between the bishop and the prefect.[98]

There was basis for the rumor. As a traditionalist embodying in word and deed the Aristotelian *aretai politikai,* "she was swift and ingenious in arguments; in action she was known for prudence and political virtue."[99] She had associated herself with the old structure of the *civitas* based on a secular civil government and on discourse, not violence, in politics. She undoubtedly shared with Orestes the conviction that the authority of the bishops should not extend to areas meant for the imperial and municipal administration. She would have remembered that the late Theophilus, notwithstanding his lust for power and his campaign against paganism in Alexandria, had not acted dictatorially but had availed himself of help and support from representatives of the emperor.[100] She had witnessed the harmonious cooperation of civil and ecclesiastical authorities. How else are we to interpret Synesius' recourse on behalf of his protégés to both Hypatia and Theophilus? Though outside the church, she always conversed freely with city officials either when she met them as she passed through the city's streets *(dia mesou tou asteos)* or when she entertained them at home. No ecclesiastic harassed her on that account or commented on her way of life, which was known to everybody. Her political independence, which manifested itself openly in public places, was respected. People knew that her wisdom, erudition, and ethical authority induced rulers to seek her counsel.

Gradually her personal and intellectual qualities enhanced her political influence as she modified her former role as "a philosopher-observer" through more active participation in the city's affairs. Owing to her support, in the years 414–415 Orestes was able to forge a kind of political party.[101] In this effort he may also have been aided by the leaders of the Jewish community; at least Socrates suggests as much: he states clearly that Orestes supported the Jews' resistance against the patriarch.[102] We may therefore assume that Hypatia, too, encouraged him to defend the Jews. She would have seen them as a group long notable for its economic and cultural contribution to the life of the city.

These observations call for further interpretation of Damascius' account contrasting Hypatia with Cyril as "the bishop of the opposing party." It appears that Cyril's partisanship developed as a political response to increasing tension between the ecclesiastical and secular authorities. There is no doubt that the emergence of Orestes' faction aroused trepidation among Cyril's adherents and other clergy. John of Nikiu offers an account of the tension and fever that seized the ecclesiastical community. Socrates also revealingly describes the mood, while Damascius, we remember, writes about Cyril's envy of Hypatia's success, with the Alexandrian elite flocking to her house. Members of Cyril's faction must have realized what a powerful ally Orestes had gained for his cause. They also knew that Hypatia was not Orestes' only supporter, that behind her stood influential acquaintances. Among them, in Alexandria at least, Cyril's party greatly feared the *archontes,* city officials, Hypatia's friends, most of whom were already Christians.[103] Hypatia's alliance with Orestes' faction may have exacerbated that fear and promoted the consolidation of Cyril's ecclesiastical party.

The fact that Orestes and Hypatia's allies were essentially a Christian group complicated the situation for Cyril and his clergy.[104] After all, Orestes was himself a Christian and the representative of a Christian state; he was backed by members of the city's Christian elite and a segment of the Christian populace who had defended him from the monks' assault—the same Alexandrians who, together with Abundantius, had favored Timothy for the bishopric.

There were additional reasons for apprehension. Cyril and his supporters realized that Hypatia enjoyed influence outside Alexandria. Not only were her disciples of high birth; they occupied high positions in the service of the empire and the church. Herculianus' brother Cyrus may by that time have gained an important post at the court of Theodosius II—at least he had become a high-ranking politician; Hesychius held the office of *dux et corrector Libyarum;* Synesius was no longer alive, but his brother Euoptius had probably already succeeded him as bishop of Ptolemais; Olympius was a wealthy landowner in Syria, on friendly terms with high-ranking politicians such as the *comes* known also to Herculianus who had become a prominent figure in Alexandria. Hypatia's influence, then, reached as far as Constantinople, Syria, and Cyrene. Her friendships and influence among imperial functionaries and hieratics of the church would surely have generated anxiety among Cyril's followers.

In the face of the social disturbances in Alexandria, Cyril could not even be sure of the conduct of Aurelian, the praetorian prefect of the years 414–416. He was, after all, Synesius' acquaintance from the times of the latter's mission to Constantinople, and the object of his literary compliments in *On Providence*.[105] Cyril and his associates might have presumed that Orestes was Aurelian's acquaintance and that he had heard about Hypatia's qualities from him or from other of Synesius' friends before coming to Alexandria. This might explain his formation of a strong friendship with Hypatia in so short a time after the beginning of his administration there.

Damascius, who knew much more about Hypatia's important position in Alexandria than we do, did not hesitate to elaborate on this point: he states briefly and unequivocally that the whole city "doted on her and worshiped her." She was also showered with civic honors.[106] Cyril could not even dream of such adulation; he was unwanted and disliked from the moment he ascended to the bishopric. He perceived his weakness, and he was afraid he might lose in the struggle against Orestes. But he also knew he had the backing of the clergy, the monks, some members of the intellectual elite (like Hierax), and, perhaps, the city council. Finally, he could count on the *pollon plethos* who had helped him in the destruction of the Jewish dwellings.

These were the men who supported the patriarch's cause, who would not hesitate to undertake action to save it. Hypatia was neither popular nor celebrated among the Alexandrian populace at large. Together with her students she separated herself from the *demos;* she did not direct her teachings to the masses, and she had no influence among them.[107] Nor were there any reasons for the pagan groups in the city to consider her an ally; they remembered her lack of interest in traditional beliefs during their most recent struggle to preserve the Hellenic religion.

Cyril's people found a way to exploit Hypatia's detachment from the common people: they devised a subtle scheme of negative propaganda among the urban mob. John of Nikiu relates that they portrayed her as a witch and imputed to her the worst type of sorcery—black magic—which drew the severest punishment not only in the legal system of the Christian empire; it was as old as the Twelve Tables.[108] Rumors of the practice of black magic spawned devastating fear among ordinary people, who were accordingly ever ready to take violent and ruthless action against sorcerers.

Alexandrians thus learned that the famous woman philosopher was in reality an abominable messenger of hell, "devoted at all times to magic, astrolabes, and instruments of music." The ecclesiastical propagandists thus imbued one tendentious little story about a sorceress with information about Hypatia's mathematical and astronomical research, her philosophical and religious interests, and anecdotes circulating about her in the city. To authenticate the information about Hypatia's forbidden practices it sufficed to refer to her father's preoccupation with astrology and magic, his writings on the interpretation of dreams, and the Alexandrian astrologists' calls at their house. Hesychius, aware of what lay at the core of the people's agitation, states unequivocally that it was astronomy that sealed her fate—understood, of course, as astrology alloyed with black magic and divination.[109]

Through such manipulations Hypatia was presented as a dangerous witch casting satanic spells on many people of the city; "she beguiled many people through [her] satanic wiles." The first to fall victim to her was "the governor of the city," Orestes; as a result of Hypatia's spells he stopped attending church and started an active "atheization" of Christian believers. He encouraged them to visit Hypatia (John of Nikiu probably means her lectures), and "he himself received the unbelievers at his house."

John of Nikiu also blames Hypatia for the Christian-Jewish conflict. Hierax, whom the Jews in the theater pointed out to Orestes as Cyril's spy and informant, is depicted as "a Christian possessing understanding and intelligence, who used to mock the pagans but was a devoted adherent of the illustrious Father, the patriarch, and was obedient to his monitions." Orestes, who sentenced Hierax to torture and the good monk Ammonius to death, was ill disposed toward "the children of the church." That is why he lent support to the Jews, who, assured of his help and assistance, refused to listen to the patriarch when he called upon them to cease their hostility toward the Christians. By means of insidious deceit they assaulted the Christians and massacred a large body of them. In revenge the Christians plundered the synagogues, turned them into churches, and expelled the Jews from the city. In the face of such decisive action, the prefect was unable to protect the Jews.

Only after settling matters with the Jews did the Christians turn against "the pagan woman," the cause of all the trouble in the city. Having related the pogrom of the Jews, John of Nikiu offers a description of Hypatia's murder. The account approximates that of Socrates in his *Ecclesiastical History,* but it differs in some particulars, including chronology: Socrates places the event some time after the disturbances in the Jewish community, while John of Nikiu presents them in direct continuity. But it is certain that the conflict with the Jews began in 414, if not in the preceding year, and that Orestes and Hypatia would have needed time to organize opposition against Cyril. Moreover, between the pogrom of the Jews and the events connected with Hypatia's death, there was the attack of the Nitrian monks on Orestes. Finally, in their accounts of the rumors circulating about Hypatia, both John of Nikiu and Socrates suggest that there must have been some interval during which the propaganda against Hypatia could take effect among the Alexandrians.

That *diabole,* the ominous and slanderous rumor about Hypatia's witchcraft and its divisive effect on the city, produced the results desired by the instigators. From that company emerged a group that resolved to kill the woman philosopher. Socrates says that they distinguished themselves by "hot-tempered disposition"; John of Nikiu calls them "a multitude of believers in God"; and Damascius refers to them as beasts rather than human beings.[110]

At the head of those who contrived the fearful plot stood— according to Socrates—a certain Peter, a church lector, perhaps a clergyman of lower holy orders. In John of Nikiu he appears as "the magistrate." John of Nikiu's version seems plausible in the light of our considerations of Hypatia's social position and her city connections. Among the city officials, the *curiales* with whom Hypatia had political and intellectual ties, there could have been individuals unsympathetic toward her, Cyril's followers. They too could have reported to the patriarch what was going on and what decisions were made in the city council, in the prefect's *officium,* or among people connected with Hypatia and Orestes.

Led by Peter, a mob executed the deed on a day in March 415, in the tenth consulship of Honorius and the sixth consulship of Theodosius II, during Lent. Hypatia was returning home, through a street whose name is unknown to us, from her customary ride in the city. She was pulled out of the chariot and dragged to the church Caesarion, a former temple of the emperor cult. There they tore off her clothes and killed her with "broken bits of pottery" *(ostrakois aneilon).*[111] Then they hauled her body outside the city to a place called Kinaron, to burn it on a pyre of sticks.[112]

In John of Nikiu's perspective, the killing of a witch was but the fulfillment of the common will of the Christians and of God himself. A group of the faithful, led by Peter, a "perfect believer in all respects in Jesus Christ," went out into the city to look for the "pagan woman"; they found her sitting "on a (lofty) chair," and thus by all appearances conducting a lecture. From here she was dragged to the church and there disgraced and stripped of her robes. Then (in a slightly different version from Socrates') she was dragged through the streets until she died. Finally, her body was carted to a place called Kinaron, where it was burned.

Among other sources, Malalas confirms that after the murder the body was burned on a pyre;[113] Hesychius offers an account similar to that of John of Nikiu, that "she was torn to pieces by the Alexandrians and her body shamefully treated and parts of it scattered all over the city."[114] Others only mention Hypatia's death without providing any details.

Relying on the most important sources and their analysis, we may thus state unequivocally that the conflict between Orestes and Cyril was concluded in a manner and for a reason known and used for ages: murder for a political purpose. The problem, which to the patriarch and his associates appeared insoluble, could be eliminated only by a criminal act. They killed a person who was the mainstay of the opposition against him, who through her authority and political connections provided support for the representative of the state authority in Alexandria contending against Cyril.

The assassination had been well contrived. After the dreadful event, Orestes was probably recalled, or he may have requested his own recall. In any case we never hear anything more about him. Certainly there are grounds to assume that he felt disgust for the city and was fearful that Hypatia's lot might become his own. With the end of the turmoil, the city calmed down. Cyril achieved his desired position in Alexandria. The imperial officials must have begun to take him seriously, since we hear of no more conflicts for the rest of his pontificate.

Only the city councillors of Alexandria tried to intervene with the emperor against the bishop. As Damascius tells us somewhat darkly, the matter was hushed because there were people at court who favored Cyril.[115] A man named Aedesius even attempted to bribe the emperor's friends. Cyril undoubtedly presented the affair as a struggle against paganism (with such of its manifestations as magic and sorcery), as official church propaganda proclaimed after all. That he did the same when coping with the highest authorities we may infer from John of Nikiu, who at the end of his account announces that after the killing of Hypatia "all the people surrendered to the patriarch Cyril and named him 'the new Theophilus'; for he destroyed the last remains of idolatry in the city."

Cyril's preventive action and his method of vindicating Hypatia's murder fell on fertile soil. During the regency of Pulcheria and the second prefecture of Aurelian, the imperial court campaigned actively against pagans and Jews.[116] Aurelian, apparently heedless of Synesius' homage in *On Providence,* made no response to the shocking death of his beloved teacher. He had become an ardent proponent of orthodoxy, a ruthless adversary of paganism, and an instigator of antipagan legislation.[117]

Synesius' letters to Hypatia in the last year of his life (*Epp.* 10, 15, 16, and 81) indicate that his relationship with her was waning. As we recall, they are filled with complaints about the lack of letters from her and about her indifference to his hard lot.[118] Hypatia apparently ceased to correspond with Synesius, possibly because she did not want to involve him in the antagonistic situation with the patriarch, whose subordinate he was. She would not have wanted to add pain to his personal and political worries.

Ultimately, of course, we can never know the reason for the weakening of relations between Hypatia and her erstwhile student. It is possible that once she had joined the struggle against the church, she turned away from her friend too hastily; for Synesius was not an admirer of Cyril, as his only letter to him (*Ep.* 12) reveals. In it he treats the youthful patriarch as an inexperienced and erring younger brother in Christ. In contrast, he refers to Theophilus with genuine deference and faithful devotion, calling him "our holy Father of holy memory," "sacred priest," "dear to God." He reminds Cyril that Theophilus, beloved by God, appointed him to be shepherd of the church notwithstanding his numerous grievances against him. This letter certainly provides no reason to suspect Synesius of being Cyril's ally.[119] But the loss of contact with Hypatia may have exacerbated Synesius' illness and contributed to his spiritual depression, the symptoms of which are observable in *Epistle* 15. Preoccupied with her political cause, Hypatia did not think about Synesius. The news of his death must have surprised her.

After repeated petitions to the court in Constantinople, the city council in Alexandria obtained some measure of punishment for Cyril. On October 5, 416, Aurelian's successor, the praetorian prefect Monaxius, issued an order that stripped Cyril of his authority over the so-called parabalanai or parabolans and demanded their reorganization.[120] The parabolans were a college of strong young men connected with the Alexandrian church whose task it was to collect the ill, disabled, and homeless in the city and place them in hospitals or church almshouses.[121] But the sources reveal that they also served as a sort of military arm of the Alexandrian patriarch, carrying out actions against his adversaries in various places and situations.

The imperial ordinance of 416 prohibited the parabolans from appearing in public places or entering the premises of the city council or its tribunals; their number was reduced from 800 to 500, and the recruitment of new members was handed over to the prefect; previously, the patriarch had appointed members of his choosing. Henceforth they were to be recruited from the class of "paupers"; those coming from the city *curiales,* from the class of *honorati,* were deprived of membership. In 418, however, the bishop regained the right to select the parabolans, and their number was increased to 600. Only the restrictions on their movements about the city remained in force.[122]

It was surely the parabolans, the patriarch's "guard," who committed the murder of Hypatia. They were the chief propagators of the falsehoods about her sorcery; it was they who appeared with the monks at Theophilus' side when he was destroying paganism in Alexandria, they who led the mob with which he attacked the Jewish quarters, and they who committed the violence at the Council of Ephesus.[123] Most of them were ignorant and uneducated, but they were obedient to their ecclesiastical leaders; hotheaded and prone to manipulation and provocation, they responded with violent actions to the popular moods of Alexandria in 414 and 415. It was they who made up the core of the ecclesiastical masses described by Socrates, manipulated the Alexandrian mob, and fanned the campaign against Hypatia. They knew nothing of the subjects she was teaching; they understood neither the principles she followed nor the values she served. Her independence and inscrutability, distance, and philosophical loftiness undoubtedly irritated them.

Contrary to the opinion of several scholars who hold that the deed was committed by monks,[124] Socrates states that the monks, terrified by popular reaction to their aggression against the prefect Orestes, took flight.[125] They went back to the desert, to their lairs—unless we accept Rougé's view that Cyril ordered some of them to join the parabolans and thus detained them in Alexandria.[126] John of Nikiu also acquits the monks of the murder, pinning the blame instead on Alexandrians who distinguished themselves by their "profound religiosity." Hesychius likewise asserts: "She was torn to pieces by the Alexandrians." In the eighth century Theophanes observes that the deed was done by "certain" people, that is, a band of the city masses; he does not as much as mention the monks. Finally, Nicephorus Callistus repeats Socrates' version of the assassination.[127] Socrates, who describes in detail the monks' assault on Orestes, surely would not have failed to mention their aggression against Hypatia; and he would have mentioned their return to Alexandria. However, the matter was taken care of by local people coming from the city's masses, subordinated to the church and manipulated by the clergy.

Like everyone else who has studied Hypatia, we are bound to take a stand on Cyril's guilt. We cannot go so far as F. Schaefer, who absolves him completely and puts the blame on Orestes.[128] And as Rougé and others rightly assert, Cyril cannot be held legally responsible for planning the murder.[129]

But Cyril must be held to account for a great deal, even if we assume that the murder was contrived and executed by the parabolans, without his knowledge. For there is no doubt that he was a chief instigator of the campaign of defamation against Hypatia, fomenting prejudice and animosity against the woman philosopher, rousing fear about the consequences of her alleged black-magic spells on the prefect, the faithful of the Christian community, and indeed the whole city.

However directly or indirectly he was involved, Cyril violated the principles of the Christian moral order, which he was bound to nurture and uphold. He could not reconcile himself to the possible eclipse of his influence. Hypatia and, through her,

Orestes exercised leadership among the elite of Alexandria. Cyril, his ambition thwarted, consumed by frustration and envy, became a dangerous man. Socrates, Hesychius, and Damascius all point to Cyril's jealousy as the cause of Hypatia's death. Of the three, Damascius makes the gravest and most specific accusations against Cyril; as proof of jealousy, he offers the anecdote about Cyril passing by Hypatia's house and observing a crowd at her door awaiting her appearance. Our reconstruction of the background and the course of events resulting in her death divest this little story of the aura of a naive fable about an evil Cyril and a noble Hypatia. It becomes a metaphoric tale about the small-mindedness and destructive passions of the bishop. We lack, however, some proof from other sources to confirm the conclusions Damascius draws from the anecdote. For he establishes a strict relation between Cyril's evil passions and desire for murder and its fulfillment. Damascius is convinced that Cyril contrived Hypatia's assassination and executed it with the help of his men.

For Socrates, envy of Hypatia's good fortune and prestige among the ruling class was the decisive cause of the murder. From the context in which he speaks about the destructive feeling of jealousy of Hypatia's "earthly" honors, it follows that he has Cyril and his party in mind even though he does not name the patriarch. Hesychius, on the other hand, provides two versions of the killing, with two different causes: one cites envy of Hypatia's wisdom and astronomical knowledge, nourished by Cyril and his supporters; the other blames "the innate rashness and tendency toward sedition among the Alexandrians."[130] Malalas reiterates that Cyril understood the psychology of the Alexandrian masses, and especially of the groups associated with him. Aware of Cyril's envy of and animosity against Hypatia, Malalas accuses the bishop of inciting the people to the crime. He states that Cyril gave the "Alexandrians" (he probably means the parabolans) freedom for action against a famous and widely respected woman of advanced age.

Socrates, usually so careful in judging evidence and attributing causes, cannot, at the end of his story of the events, resist expressing indignation against Cyril and his church: "This affair brought not the least opprobrium, not only upon Cyril, but also upon the whole Alexandrian church." But he also observes that the Alexandrians were far more inclined toward anarchy and disturbances than the people of any other city.[131] Similarly, as Hesychius reflects on the murder, he observes that it was not the first assassination committed by the people of Alexandria. They had slain two bishops: George, the Arian bishop of Alexandria, appointed by the emperor Constantius, who was killed in 361 during the reign of Julian the Apostate; and Proterius, also an imperial appointee, who was murdered in 457. Their bodies, like Hypatia's, were dragged all over the city and then burned.[132] Other ancient sources follow Socrates and Hesychius in confessing an inability to explain the Alexandrian propensity to violence and crime.[133]

But the murder of Hypatia, a sixty-year-old woman, widely esteemed for her wisdom and ethical virtue, was not only an act of hatred but also a criminal offense warranting a swift and severe response from those charged with upholding the law. As Damascius asserts, that response never came; those who committed the crime went unpunished and brought notable disgrace upon their city.[134]

It is not surprising that the sources on Hypatia are so few, and so sparing and generally oblique in their accounts. One reason is surely the esoteric nature of her teaching (cultivated by her disciples). But the most important reason is that as early as the fourth century Christian historians had achieved predominance, and most likely they were ashamed to write about her fate. Although Damascius, one of the few remaining pagan authors, expresses horror at the thought of her last moments and claims that the Alexandrians remembered the event long afterward,[135] others were not inclined to inform posterity about this painful event in the history of Alexandria and the Alexandrian church.

A cover-up campaign was orchestrated to protect the perpetrators, affiliated with the church, who murdered a person well disposed toward Christians. We contend against this silence when from the extant fragments we undertake to reconstruct the life and achievements of Hypatia.

CONCLUSION

With a view of Hypatia's life reclaimed from historical fragments we can see, more clearly than before, the common denominator of the literary constructs and portraits of Hypatia conceived over the last two centuries: all have used the figure of Hypatia to articulate their attitude toward Christianity, the church, its clergy, the patriarch Cyril, and so on. And, as we recall, this attitude was not purely negative. For Leconte de Lisle, Roero di Saluzzo, and Mario Luzi, Hypatia is a heroine and martyr, but her death at the hands of Christians (Saluzzo provides a variant) does not mark the end of antiquity. Her martyrdom offers a synthesis of the world of Greek values with the truths and the logos of emergent Christianity. In the last pages of Charles Kingsley's book, Hypatia even converts and becomes a confessor of the new religion. Her conversion, however, does not alter the author's view of the historical necessity of the fall of the old religions.

Kingsley's position is representative of the dominant trend in the legend, the Enlightenment or rational current, which presented Hypatia as an innocent victim of a fanatical and predatory new religion. From Toland and Voltaire to contemporary feminists, Hypatia has become a symbol both of sexual freedom and of the decline of paganism—and, with it, the waning of free thought, natural reason, freedom of inquiry. Always beautiful and young, she denoted through her death a turning point in the history of Europe, which after the expulsion of the Greek gods and the Greek notion of a harmonious cosmos had to adjust to new forms and structures imposed by the Christian church.

The legend will continue to unfold along its own course, according to tastes and fashions, as we can observe in the latest historical novels on Hypatia (Zitelmann, Ferretti, Marcel). For those who choose to restrict their focus to the actual historical sources, it is possible to sketch out a clear profile of Hypatia, undistorted by ahistorical idealization. We have established that Hypatia was born around A.D. 355, and not, as customarily held, around 370. When she died in 415 she was of an advanced age, around sixty years old. Thus there appears to be no legitimate support for the picture of Hypatia, at the hour of her horrid death, as a young girl, endowed with a body worthy of Aphrodite, provoking the murderers' sadism and lust.

She was a resident of Alexandria, from a prominent family. Her father was a well-known scientist, a member of the Museion, a writer, a philosopher interested in Hermetic and Orphic texts. Theon's scholarship (and that of his daughter) centered on eminent Alexandrian predecessors, mathematicians and astronomers. We learn from Hesychius of Miletus that as the father was writing commentaries on Euclid and Ptolemy, Hypatia was busy with the works of Apollonius of Perge, Diophantus, and Ptolemy. It has been always assumed that her studies of these authors have not survived. But Alan Cameron asserts that not all of Hypatia's texts are lost; editions of Ptolemy's *Almagest* and *Handy Tables,* now available, were probably arranged and prepared by Hypatia. It is also possible that she edited and annotated Diophantus' extant books.

Philosophy was Hypatia's other interest. Thanks to the reminiscences of her disciple Synesius in his correspondence, we know far more about her philosophical teaching than about her mathematical and astronomical research. In her home in Alexandria she formed an intellectual circle composed of disciples who came to study privately, some of them for many years. They arrived from Alexandria, from elsewhere in Egypt, and from Syria, Cyrene, and Constantinople. They were from wealthy and influential families; in time they attained posts of state and ecclesiastical eminence.

Around their teacher these students formed a community based on the Platonic system of thought and interpersonal ties. They called the knowledge passed on to them by their "divine guide" mysteries. They held it secret, refusing to share it with people of lower social rank, whom they regarded as incapable of comprehending divine and cosmic matters. Besides, the path on which Hypatia led them to divine existence was indescribable; following the path required mental effort and will, ethical strength and a desire for the infinite; its end was silence, mute ecstasy, contemplation that could not be expressed.

Hypatia's private classes and public lectures also included mathematics and astronomy, which primed the mind for speculation on higher epistemological levels. Her lectures took place either at her house (where they sometimes attracted crowds of admirers) or in the city's lecture halls. Occasionally she participated in the activities of the polis, serving as an esteemed adviser on current issues to both municipal and visiting imperial officials. She possessed great moral authority; all our sources agree that she was a model of ethical courage, righteousness, veracity, civic devotion, and intellectual prowess. The virtue most honored by her contemporaries was her sophrosyne, which colored both her conduct and her inner qualities; it manifested itself in sexual abstinence (she remained a virgin to the end of her life), in modest dress (philosophical tribon), in moderate living, and in a dignified attitude toward her students as well as men in power.

These rigorous moral principles, when enrolled in the service of the secular faction in the conflict between the patriarch Cyril and the prefect Orestes, aroused alarm and fear in ecclesiastical circles. The church authorities realized that they faced an experienced individual endowed with considerable authority, exerting extensive influence, determined in the defense of her convictions; in addition, through her influential disciples she might win support for Orestes among people close to the emperor.

The conflict between Christian parties reached alarming proportions in the years 414–415. Orestes doggedly resisted Cyril's attempts to encroach upon the sovereignty of the civil power. He remained intransigent even when Cyril tried to make peace. Suspicion arose among Cyril's adherents that Hypatia, a friend of the prefect, had incited and sustained his resistance. The patriarch felt threatened, and people from various groups connected with the church decided to aid him. Monks assaulted Orestes, and Cyril's associates skillfully mounted and spread rumors about Hypatia's studies of magic and her satanic spell on the prefect, "on God's people," and on the entire city. The struggle between the patriarch and the prefect over political power and the influence of the church on secular affairs ended in her death. Men in Cyril's employment assassinated Hypatia. It was a political murder provoked by long-standing conflicts in Alexandria.[1] Through this criminal act a powerful supporter of Orestes was eliminated. Orestes himself not only gave up his struggle against the patriarch but left Alexandria for good. The ecclesiastical faction paralyzed his followers with fear and pacified the city; only the city councillors attempted—with meager effect—to intervene with the emperor.

Hypatia's death had no connection with the antipagan policy pursued by Cyril and his church at that time. Cyril (if not Peter Mongos) in the first years of his rule merely obliterated the temple of Isis in Méneuthé near Canopus, replacing it with the cult of Christian saints (Cyrus and John).[2] He did not persecute pagans in Alexandria itself (there he was more interested in heretics and Jews). Not until the years 420–430—a considerable time after Hypatia's death—did he launch an assault on pagan thought and practices in his treatise *Contra Julianum,* which attacked Julian the Apostate's *Contra Galilaeos.*[3]

In any case it would have been difficult to challenge or persecute Hypatia on the basis of her paganism, for unlike her contemporary fellow philosophers, she was not an active, devoted pagan. She did not cultivate Neoplatonic theurgic philosophy, visit temples, or resist their conversion into Christian churches. Indeed, she sympathized with Christianity and protected her Christian students. With her tolerance and consummate grasp of metaphysical questions, she assisted them in achieving spiritual and religious integrity. Two of her students became bishops. Pagans and Christians studying with her congregated in friendship. During the rule of Cyril's predecessor, Theophilus, the church had not interfered with her activity in the city, recognizing her views and her position. Thus Cyril's people, deprived of the opportunity to attack her on the grounds that she was a pagan, accused her of witchcraft, of sorcery. We therefore cannot join with those who lament Hypatia as "the last of the Hellenes" or who maintain that Hypatia's death marked the demise of Alexandrian science and philosophy. Pagan religiosity did not expire with Hypatia, and neither did mathematics and Greek philosophy. After her death the philosopher Hierocles initiated a rather salient development of eclectic Neoplatonism in Alexandria.[4] Until the Arab invasion philosophers continued to elaborate the teachings of Plato, Aristotle (whose popularity increased in Alexandria during that time), and Neoplatonists extending from Plotinus to their own contemporaries. In keeping with the Alexandrian tradition, they continued to advance mathematics and astronomy. The Alexandrian school achieved its greatest success at the turn of the fifth and sixth centuries in the persons of Ammonius, Damascius (associated with Alexandria and Athens), Simplicius, Asclepius, Olympiodorus, and John Philoponus.[5]

Paganism also persisted, and to a degree even flowered, under the "holy men" of Neoplatonism who combined Late Platonic philosophy with ritual and sacerdotal service to the gods.[6] Holding dear old cults, theurgy, and divination, they cultivated "Egyptian wisdom," studied hieroglyphics, revived old Greek and Egyptian rites, and attracted disciples. These philosophers came from the school of Horapollon the Older, who lived in the time of Theodosius II: Haraiskos, Asclepiades, Horapollon the Younger, and their contemporaries, such as Sarapion and Asclepiodotos.[7]

Hypatia stands at the threshold of those philosophic-religious developments of the fifth century that greatly attract today's scholars of late antiquity.[8] The intellectual circle created by her in the fourth century, consisting of the inspired teacher and her disciples, had in common the same fundamental goal that guided the "holy men" of Alexandrian Neoplatonism in the next century: the consistent aspiration (with allowance for all the differences in epistemological methods) to achieve religious experience as the essential ideal of philosophy.

Abbreviations
Sources
Notes
Index

ABBREVIATIONS

AG	*Anthologia Graeca*
AP	*Anthologia Palatina*
BIFAO	*Bulletin de l'Institut français d'archéologie orientale*
Bregman	J. Bregman, *Synesius of Cyrene, Philosopher-Bishop* (Berkeley, 1982)
Cameron (1993)	A. Cameron and J. Long with a contribution by L. Sherry, *Barbarians and Politics at the Court of Arcadius* (Berkeley)
CCAG	*Catalogus Codicum Astrologorum Graecorum*
CH	*Corpus Hermeticum*
Chron.	*The Chronicle of John, Bishop of Nikiu,* trans. R. H. Charles (Oxford, 1916)
Chronogr.	John Malalas, *Chronographia*
Chuvin	Pierre Chuvin, *A Chronicle of the Last Pagans* (Cambridge, Mass., 1990)
Crawford	W. S. Crawford, *Synesius the Hellene* (London, 1901)
C.Th.	Codex Theodosianus
Dam.	Damascius, fragments and *Epitome Photiana,* in *Damascii Vitae Isidori Reliquiae,* ed. C. Zintzen (Hildesheim, 1967)
D.L.	Diogenes Laertius, *Lives of Eminent Philosophers*
Ep.	*Synesii Cyrenensis Epistolae,* ed. A. Garzya (Rome, 1979); also in *Opere di Sinesio di Cirene, epistole, operette* (Turin, 1989)
Fowden (1979)	G. Fowden, "Pagan Philosophers in Late Antique Society" (Diss. Oxford)

Garzya (1979) and (1980)	A. Garzya, ed., *Synesii Cyrenensis Epistolae* (Rome, 1979) and *Opera di Sinesio di Cirene* (Turin, 1989)
GRBS	*Greek, Roman and Byzantine Studies*
Haas	J. C. Haas, "Late Roman Alexandria: Social Structure and Intercommunal Conflict in the Entrepôt of the East" (Ph.D. diss., University of Michigan, 1988)
HE	*Historia Ecclesiastica*
Hoche	R. Hoche, "Hypatia die Tochter Theons," *Philologus* 15 (1860)
JHS	*Journal of Hellenic Studies*
Lacombrade (1951)	Lacombrade, *Synésios de Cyrène: Hellen et chrétien* (Paris)
LSJ	H. G. Liddell, R. Scott, and H. S. Jones, eds., *A Greek-English Lexicon*
Meyer	W. A. Meyer, *Hypatia von Alexandrien. Ein Beitrag zur Geschichte des Neuplatonismus* (Heidelberg, 1886)
Mogenet (1985)	J. Mogenet and A. Tihon, eds., *Le "Grand Commentaire" de Theon d'Alexandrie aux tables faciles de Ptolémée* (Vatican, 1978 and 1985)
Neugebauer (1975)	O. Neugebauer, *A History of Ancient Mathematical Astronomy,* 3 vols. (Berlin and New York)
Penella	R. J. Penella, *Greek Philosophers and Sophists in the Fourth Century A.D.* (Liverpool, 1990)
PG	*Patrologia Graeca*
PRLE	*Prosopography of the Later Roman Empire*
RE	*Paulys Real-Encyclopädie der classischen Altertumswissenschaft*
REG	*Revue des études grecques*
Rist	J. M. Rist, "Hypatia," *Phoenix* 19 (1965)
Roques (1987)	D. Roques, *Synésios de Cyrène et la Cyrènaïque du Bas-Empire,* Etudes d'antiquités africaines (Paris)
Roques (1989)	D. Roques, *Etudes sur la correspondence de Synésios de Cyrène* (Brussels)
Rougé (1990)	J. Rougé, "La politique de Cyrille d'Alexandrie et le meurtre d'Hypatie," *Cristianesiono nella storia* 11, 485–504
Tihon (1978)	See Mogenet (1985)
VS	Eunapius, *Lives of the Sophists*

SOURCES

Historians of the late Roman empire and the Christian church since Constantine the Great have, until recently, written little about Hypatia, and their accounts tend to be repetitious and trite. Most such works, apparently following the example of Edward Gibbon in *The History of the Decline and Fall of the Roman Empire* (vol. 5 [London, 1898], pp. 109–110), confine discussion of Hypatia's life and achievements to a narrative of the events connected with her death in A.D. 415, in the context of ideological strife during the empire's transition to a Christian state.

The first monographs dealing with Hypatia appeared in the second half of the nineteenth century and are cited in Chapter I. Although they offer interesting analyses and serious arguments, they are obsolete; they interpret the historical material about Hypatia subjectively, relying heavily on the evolving legend; and they are overburdened with general material on Alexandrian history and culture at the expense of reliable information about Hypatia herself.

In our own day scholars have produced numerous articles and treatises on the woman philosopher. These include J. M. Rist, "Hypatia," *Phoenix* 19 (1965):214–225; C. Lacombrade, "Hypatie: La mythe et l'historie," *Bulletin de la Societé Toulousaine d'études classique* 166 (1972):5–20; E. Evrard, "A quel titre Hypatie enseigne-t-elle la philosophie?" *REG* 90 (1977):69–74; V. Lambropoulou in *Platon* 29 (1977):65–78 (summary in English: "Hypatia, the Alexandrian Philosopher," *Hypatia* 1 [1984]:3–11); R. J. Penella, "When Was Hypatia Born?" *Historia* 33 (1984):126–128; D. Shanzer, "Merely a Cynic Gesture," *Rivista di filologia e di istruzione classica* 113 (1985):61–66; and G. Arrigoni, "Tra le donne dell' antichità: Considerazioni e ricognizioni," *Atti del Convegno nazionale di studi su la donna nel mondo antico, Torino, 21–23 aprile 1986* (Turin, 1987), pp. 63–71. Worthy of special attention is Alan Cameron's essay "Isidore of Miletus and Hypatia: On the Editing of Mathematical Texts," *GRBS* 31 (1990):103–127; it offers new insight into up-to-date findings on Hypatia's (and her father's) commentaries on Ptolemy's *Almagest. Barbarians and Politics at the Court of Arcadius,* by A. Cameron and J. Long, with a contribution by L. Sherry (Berkeley, 1993), is devoted to Synesius of Cyrene but offers fresh views and reflections on Hypatia's life and thought. My great debt to these scholars becomes apparent in the notes. J. Rougé's article "La politique de Cyrille d'Alexandrie et le meurtre d'Hypatie," *Cristianesiono nella storia* 11 (1990):485–504, presents the most recent interpretation of the events connected with Hypatia's death. I received the article through the courtesy of Professor St. Gero (Tübingen) after completion of the Polish edition of this book. It was gratifying to discover that the author's views on the death of Hypatia concur with mine. See also a publication to which I had no access: P. Giorgiades, *Une martyre paienne: La mort d'Hypatie* (L'Atelier d'Alexandrie, 1982).

Despite considerable interest in Hypatia, no scholarly book has been devoted to her for more than a century. W. A. Meyer's modest *Hypatia von Alexandrien. Ein Beitrag zur Geschichte des Neuplatonismus* (Heidelberg, 1886) has yet to be replaced by a more substantial work. Unfortunately, I was unable to consult G. Beretta's *Ipazia d'Alessandria* (Rome, 1993) before sending my manuscript to the publisher to be translated. The dearth of scholarship reflects the extraordinary paucity of sources. In many cases information is limited to a few sentences, and the most extensive texts about her, which promise to make up for the deficiencies of knowledge, are little more than compilations of heterogeneous data of unequal equality, some significant, some tendentious, and some resisting interpretation.

The most important and most valuable intelligence about Hypatia's life comes from the *Ecclesiastical History* of Socrates Scholasticus (ca. 379–450), her contemporary. (On Socrates see *The Ecclesiastical History of Socrates Scholasticus: A Select Library of Nicene and Post-Nicene Fathers of the Christian Church,* ed. P. Schaff and H. Wace, II [Michigan, 1952], pp. viii–xvi. See also W. von Christs, *Geschichte der Griechischen Literatur* [Munich, 1924], p. 1433f. = *Handbuch der Altertumswissenschaft,* VII.2, 2; and G. F. Chesnut, *The First Christian Histories: Eusebius, Socrates, Sozomen, Theodoret, Evagrius* [Paris, 1977], pp. 168–190. This church historian, a lawyer from Constantinople, whose opus is a continuation of the *History of the Church* by Eusebius of Caesarea, devotes one chapter to Hypatia.) Although Socrates' account of Hypatia is brief, his data are historically reliable. As students of his writings point out, he was well informed about political and ecclesiastical developments in the empire, and his knowledge of Hypatia was most likely derived from eyewitnesses. Some of these were teachers of rhetoric, such as Ammonias and Helladius, who, before they moved to Constantinople, were teachers of literature and priests of pagan cults in Alexandria. There can be no doubt that they remembered Hypatia well and talked about her in Constantinople. By putting her murder firmly in the context of the events of 412–415, he helps us to ascertain the causes of her death. Certainly, he exposes the close involvement of the Alexandrian church. Echoing Socrates' account of Hypatia's life and death is the sixth-century *Historia Tripartita Ecclesiastica* (XI.12; *CSEL,* LXXI, 643–644), which originated in the circle around Aurelius Cassiodorus; it is a compilation of the church histories of Socrates, Sozomen, and Theodoret of Cyrrhus, based on the translation of these works by Epiphanius.

Philostorgius of Cappadocia, another contemporary of Hypatia (born around 368), describes her in a few sentences in his *Ecclesiastical History* (VIII.9; *GCS,* 21; *Historia Ecclesiastica,* ed. J. Bidez, 3d ed. [Berlin, 1981], p. 111), another continuation of Eusebius' *History.* Philostorgius, whose work we know from Photius' summaries, was an Arian, a follower of Eunomius (Bidez, pp. cvi–cxiii). Clearly biased, he wove Hypatia's fate into the story of the struggle between the Arians and the orthodox followers of the Nicene Creed, blaming the latter for her death. Apart from this highly controversial allegation, Philostorgius supplies a few valuable facts about Hypatia's education and her competence in the exact sciences.

In his *Chronographia,* which covers the history of the world from its creation until 565, the Antiochian chronicler John Malalas (491–578) includes two extremely interesting sentences about Hypatia (*Chronogr.,* XIV [p. 359 Dindorf] = *PG,* 97, p. 536A). (On Malalas and his works see K. Krumbacher, *Geschichte der byzantinischen Literatur,* 2d ed. [Munich, 1897], pp. 325–334; also H. Hunger, *Die hochsprachliche profane Literatur der Byzantiner,* I [Munich, 1978], pp. 319–326 = *Handbuch der Altertumswissenschaft,* XII, 5, 1; and G. Downey, *A History of Antioch in Syria* [Princeton, 1961], pp. 37–40, p. 192ff.) These contain essential information about Hypatia's life span, her fame and popularity in the city, and some clues about the perpetrators of the murder. Malalas lived close enough to the events to transmit credible intelligence about them. He also furnishes important data about Hypatia's father, Theon.

A short sixth-century biography of Hypatia by Hesychius of Miletus (known as the Illustrious) in his lexicon of Greek writers, *Onomatologus,* has not survived in its original form but has been reconstructed from excerpts preserved by later authors (*Hesychii Milesi Onomatologi quae supersunt cum prolegomenis,* ed. J. Flach [Leipsig, 1882]). The entry on Hypatia (p. 219 Flach) suggests the titles of Hypatia's writings and tells about her mathematical talent and astronomical knowledge. Hesychius includes a surprising tidbit about Hypatia's marriage to the Alexandrian philosopher Isidore; this fanciful rumor has been eagerly repeated by modern historians—for example, by S. Le Nain de Tillemont and by P. Tannery, a student of sources on the history of Hypatia.

The seventh-century *Chronicle* by John of Nikiu, available as *The Chronicle of John, Bishop of Nikiu,* trans. R. H. Charles (Oxford, 1916), is of exceptional importance. The bishop of Nikiu in Lower Egypt, born during the capture of Egypt by the Arabs, wrote a history of the world from Adam to his own time. His *Chronicle* constitutes a valuable source for the history of both Byzantium and Byzantine Egypt. The work has survived through an Ethiopian edition copied from an Arabic text. This circumstance, however, does not diminish its value, as it is the product of a local author who had access to records of the Alexandrian church, no longer extant.

John of Nikiu's *Chronicle* is the only extant source that presents Hypatia in an unfavorable light, as a pagan philosopher devoted to occult practices: astrology, sorcery, and divination (*Chron.* 84.87–103; pp. 100–102 Charles). His work, next to Socrates', stands forth as the most substantial and most cohesive source for the recreation of the events connected with Hypatia's activity in Alexandria and the circumstances of her death.

Most historians seeking information about Hypatia in the nineteenth and early twentieth centuries consulted the *Suda,* a well-known Byzantine lexicon of the tenth century (s.v. Hypatia 4 [644.1–646.5 Adler] = Dam. frags. 102 and 276 [pp. 77, 79, 81, 219 Zintzen]). The first part of the entry on Hypatia relies mainly on Hesychius, the second part on Damascius' *Life of Isidore.* (On the origin of the entry in *Suda* see P. Tannery, "L'article de Suidas sur Hypatia," *Annales de la Faculté des lettres de Bordeaux* 2 [1880]:197–200; J. R. Asmus, "Zur Rekonstruktion von Damascius Leben des Isidorus," *Byzantische Zeitschrift* 18 [1909]:424–480 and 19 [1910]):265–284; K. Praechter, *RE,* 9[1] [1914], col. 242, s.v. Hypatia.) The influences of Socrates and Philostorgius are also discernible.

Damascius' *Life of Isidore* was first reconstructed by R. Asmus,

Das Leben des Philosophen Isidoros von Damaskios aus Damascos (Leipzig, 1911). There is now also available an edition by C. Zintzen, *Damascii Vitae Isidori Reliquiae* (Hildesheim, 1967). Isidore, a Late Platonic philosopher from Alexandria, a disciple of Proclus, was born in 450 (*PRLE*, II, pp. 628–631, s.v. Isidorus 5; *Der kleine Pauly*, II, 1460 [H. Dörrie]). About a year after his death around 526, his disciple Damascius, the last scholarch of the Academy, wrote a biography of his teacher. (On Damascius see *PRLE*, II, pp. 342–343; A. Cameron, "The Last Days of the Academy at Athens," *Proceedings of the Cambridge Philological Society* 195 [1969]:8–28.) Thus there is a hiatus of two full generations between Hypatia's and Isidore's deaths. Their backgrounds, however, were very similar. He was raised and educated in Alexandria in the circles of the Neoplatonic philosophers Heraiscus and Asclepiades. Their father, Herapollon the Elder, lived in the times of Theodosius II and was a contemporary of Hypatia. (See G. Fowden, "The Pagan Holy Man in Late Antique Society," *JHS* 102 [1982]:46–48; Chuvin, pp. 106–107, 110–111.)

The *Life of Isidore,* considered the best source on Alexandria's pagan history in the fifth century and the beginning of the sixth, is an apology for a fading civilization, its systems of beliefs and thought. But though fundamental to the reconstruction of the pagan milieu in Alexandria, it provides no thoughtful characterization of Hypatia's personality, no penetrating description of her philosophy, no review of her scholarly writings. Any noteworthy information about Hypatia must be extracted from the praise of her virtues, manners, and political skills. Damascius' highly compressed and occasionally inconsistent account of her demands close and critical reading and comparison with other sources; nevertheless, as the longest text about Hypatia it remains one that no scholar can ignore.

In the middle Byzantine period Theophanes (around 752–818) wrote a brief account of Hypatia's death (*Chronographia,* I; p. 82.16 De Boor). Finally, in the late Byzantine period Nicephorus Callistus Xanthopulos (around 1253–1335) produced a derivative description of her life and death, a compilation of earlier sources based primarily on Socrates, in his *Ecclesiastical History* (XIV.16.469–470; *PG,* 146.1105–08B).

The surviving ancient accounts of Hypatia—even the better ones such as those of Socrates, Damascius, and John of Nikiu—are insufficient for a reconstruction of her life without the information provided about her and her disciples in the writings of Synesius of Cyrene, especially in his letters addressed to Hypatia and to his friends. Despite numerous gaps, these writings are of unquestionable value, for Synesius knew Hypatia intimately and maintained a connection with her throughout his mature life. (On Synesius, besides Cameron (1993), see W. S. Crawford, *Synesius the Hellen* [London, 1901]; C. Lacombrade, *Synésios de Cyrène: Hellen et chrétien* [Paris, 1951]; J. Bregman, *Synesius of Cyrene: Philosopher-Bishop* [Berkeley, 1982].)

Other Learned Women of Late Antiquity

A host of remarkable women in antiquity and in the early Byzantine period engaged in the study of philosophy.[1] The Neoplatonic era produced a great number of women devoted to philosophy. We know little about most of them beyond their names. Two Roman matrons, Chione and Gemina, were patrons of Plotinus in Rome; Gemina's daughter, named after her mother, was Plotinus' student.[2] Another student of Plotinus, Amphiclea, married the son of the philosopher Iamblichus;[3] Porphyry's wife, Marcella, also demonstrated interest in philosophy.[4] The woman philosopher Arete, to whom Iamblichus addressed a letter on the virtue of moderation, was a member of his circle.[5]

The best-known, most original, and most influential woman philosopher was Sosipatra. She lived in the first half of the fourth century, teaching philosophy in Pergamon. Eunapius so admired Sosipatra's wisdom that he included a portrait of her in his *Lives of the Philosophers and Sophists.*[6] R. J. Penella, in his study of Eunapius, follows the latter in asserting that Sosipatra combined mystical Platonism and theurgy.[7] According to Eunapius, during her childhood Sosipatra was initiated in Chaldean practices by two foreigners and thus acquired the power of divination and communion with divine beings. She in turn endowed her students with such gifts in her private philosophical school in Pergamon, which enjoyed greater success than the neighboring school of the famous Aedesius, Iamblichus' disciple.

Plutarch's daughter Asclepigeneia also achieved celebrity as a philosopher.[8] Hypatia's contemporary and a master at the Athenian Academy, Plutarch introduced his daughter to the secrets of theurgy and Chaldean magic; she in turn bequeathed them to the eminent fifth-century philosopher Proclus, Syrianus' successor as director of the Academy. Some early scholars, including H. Druon, held that Hypatia had studied philosophy in Athens and was Asclepigeneia's student.[9]

Alexandria produced a number of pagan and Christian women renowned for their learning. Among the former was the daughter of the philosopher Olympiodorus; Proclus studied with her when he visited Alexandria in the mid-fifth century, and Olympiodorus very much wanted him to marry her.[10] Aedesia, a philosopher in her own right in the second half of the fifth century, became the wife and mother of philosophers. In his *Life of Isidore* Damascius describes her as "the best and the most beautiful of all Alexandrian women."[11] Aedesia married Hermeias, a Neoplatonic philosopher, although her relative Syranius, Plutarch's successor at the Academy in Athens, wanted her to marry Proclus.[12] With Hermeias,[13] an appointed teacher in Alexandria on a salary from the city, she had two sons, the future famed philosophers Ammonius and Heliodorus.[14] After her husband's death she took them to Athens, where she entrusted their education to Proclus. Of the two sons, Ammonius became the greater philosopher and, like his father, was granted the chair of philosophy by the city. His students included Damascius and other more or less known Alexandrian and Athenian philosophers. At Aedesia's funeral Damascius eulogized her as a universally admired woman.

Most of the learned Alexandrian Christian women, such as the ascetic St. Theodora,[15] the martyr Eugenia,[16] and St. Maria the Egyptian,[17] were granted high status in Christian hagiography. Another Hypatia of Alexandria, a widow, is mentioned in a decree of 455 by the emperor Marcianus, which granted widows, nuns, and women performing church functions the right to bestow their property on the church and the clergy.[18] That Hypatia, characterized in the decree as "a woman of most distinguished memory," had made just such a bequest.

Although there is of course no connection between this widow and our Hypatia, some ties do link the latter with Catherine, Alexandria's most beloved and best-known saint and martyr.[19] Students of the legend of Catherine have noted that her story, which began to take shape around the eighth century, contains motifs derived from Hypatia's biography.[20] Catherine appears in her *passiones* not only as a young, beautiful virgin but also as a scholar proficient in geometry, mathematics, and astronomy, devoted to the wisdom of the Greeks. Her persecutor, the emperor Maxentius (as the author of the *Life* calls him), invited fifty of the most distinguished rhetoricians and philosophers from throughout the empire, commanding them to prove Catherine's ignorance and the folly of her religious beliefs. In the presence of the emperor, Catherine countered the wise men's arguments and in addition converted them to Christianity. Nevertheless, the emperor sentenced her to torture and death. The legend connects the events with the persecution of Christians during the reign of Diocletian.

B. A. Myrsilides provides an exceptionally interesting piece of information that may help to confirm scholars' views on the connection between the legend of St. Catherine and the historical Hypatia.[21] Myrsilides writes that in Asia Minor, near the ancient town of Laodicea on the banks of the river Pyramos, close to today's Denizli, village elders showed him the ruins of a church and a much-stained inscription commemorating the dedication of the church to "St. Hypatia Catherine"; perhaps Catherine was this Hypatia's middle name.

NOTES

I. The Literary Legend of Hypatia

1. J. Toland, *Tetradymus,* chap. 3 (London, 1720), p. 103.

2. T. Lewis, *The History of Hypatia* (London, 1721); I have not seen it. C. P. Goujet represents a similar position in "Dissertation sur Hypatie où l'on justifie Saint Cyrille d'Alexandrie sur la mort de cette savante," in P. Desmolets, *Continuation des Mémoires de littérature et d'histoire,* V (Paris, 1749), pp. 138–191.

3. Voltaire, *Mélanges,* Bibliothèque de la Pléiade, 152 (Paris, 1961), pp. 1104 and 1108. On eighteenth-century philosophy see, among others, P. Gau, *The Enlightenment: An Interpretation,* I: *The Rise of Modern Paganism* (New York, 1967).

4. In *Oeuvres complètes de Voltaire,* VII: *Dictionnaire philosophique* (Paris, 1835), pp. 700, 701. Voltaire also writes about Hypatia in the treatise *De la paix perpétuelle* (1769), describing her as "de l'ancienne religion égyptienne" and spinning an improbable tale about her death. See R. Asmus, "Hypatia in Tradition und Dichtung," *Studien zur vergleichenden Literaturgeschichte* 7 (1907):26–27.

5. E. Gibbon, *The Decline and Fall of the Roman Empire* (London, 1898), pp. 109–110.

6. M. R. Lefkowitz expresses a similar view in *Women in Greek Myth* (Baltimore, 1986), p. 108.

7. In the edition of Gotha (1807), p. 76.

8. Edgard Pich, *Leconte de Lisle et sa création poetique: Poèmes antiques et Poèmes barbares* (1852–1874) (Lille, 1974), pp. 160ff.; *Oeuvres de Leconte de Lisle, Poèmes antiques* (Paris, 1897), p. 97.

9. Leconte de Lisle shared this view with other writers and literary theorists of the period, including F. R. Chateaubriand, P. Proudhon, E. Renan, Numa-Denis Fustel de Coulanges (Pich, *Leconte de Lisle,* p. 186 and nn. 83 and 86).

10. Pich, *Leconte de Lisle,* p. 160 n. 8.

11. Ibid., p. 165: "Le martyre d'Hypatie a été considéré comme l'une des manifestations les plus claire du fanatisme catolique."

12. *Oeuvres de Leconte de Lisle,* pp. 275–289.

13. G. de Nerval, *Nouvelles,* I: *Les Filles du feu. Angélique* (1854; reprint, Paris, 1931), p. 32: "La bibliothèque d'Alexandrie et le Serapéon, ou maison de secours, qu'en faisait parti, avaient été brulés et détruits au quatrième siècle par les chrétiens—qui en outre massacrèrent dans les rues la célèbre Hypatie, philosophe pythagoricienne." C.-P. de Lasteyrie included a life story of Hypatia in *Sentences de Sextius* (Paris, 1843), pp. 273–304, under the characteristic title *Vie d'Hypatie, femme célèbre, professeur de philosophie, dans le deuxième siècle à l'école d'Alexandrie,* in which he laid heavy charges against Cyril.

14. M. Barrès, *Sous l'oeil des barbares,* 2d ed. (Paris, 1904), preface, p. 6.

15. Ibid., p. 13 and passim to p. 58.

16. I use here the third edition (London, 1906).

17. H. von Schubert, "Hypatia von Alexandrien in Wahrheit und Dichtung," *Preussische Jahrbücher* 124 (1906):42–60; B. Merker, "Die historischen Quellen zu Kingsleys Roman 'Hypatia' " (Diss. Würzburg, 1909–10); Asmus in *Studien der vergleichenden Literaturgeschichte* 7 (1907), pp. 30–35. Asmus also writes about German authors imitating Kingsley (pp. 35–44). Kingsley's book is also discussed by S. Chitty, *The Beast and the Monk: A Life of Charles Kingsley* (New York, 1975), pp. 151–156.

18. J. W. Draper, *History of the Intellectual Development of Europe* (New York, 1869), pp. 238–244. On Draper see *Dictionary of Scientific Biography,* IV (New York, 1971), pp. 181–183.

19. B. Russell, *History of Western Philosophy and Its Connection with*

Political and Social Circumstances from the Earliest Times to the Present Day (London, 1946), p. 387.

20. The contents of the work and data on it are collected by G. Arrigoni, "Tra le donne dell' antichità: Considerazioni e ricognizioni," in *Atti del Convegno nazionale di studi su la donna nel mondo antico, Torino, 21–23 aprile 1986* (Turin, 1987), pp. 68–69.

21. Today, too, we find Hypatia presented as a defender of the faith and confused with Saint Catherine. See, for example, R. Richardson, *The Star Lovers* (New York, 1967), writing of Hypatia on p. 173 that she "died defending the Christians. She is followed by Catharina, an extremely learned young woman of noble family who died in A.D. 307, defending the Christians." See the discussion later in this chapter.

22. C. Pascal, "Ipazia," in *Figure e caratteri (Lucrezio, L'Ecclesiaste, Seneca, Ipazia, Giosue Carducci, Giuseppe Garibaldi)* (Milan, 1908), pp. 143–196.

23. G. Pampaloni, "La poesia religiosa del Mutamento," introduction to M. Luzi, *Libro di Ibazia e Il messagero* (Milan, 1978), p. 14.

24. I need mention only Lawrence Durrell's reference to Hypatia in *The Alexandria Quartet*. He sings his beloved Alexandria thus: "Walking those streets again in my imagination I knew once more that they spanned, not merely human history, but the whole biological scale of the heart's affections—from the painted ecstasies of Cleopatra (strange that the vine should be discovered here, near Taposiris) to the bigotry of Hypatia (withered vine-leaves, martyr's kisses)"; *Clea* (London and Boston, 1968), p. 660.

25. A. Zitelmann, *Hypatia* (Weinheim and Basel, 1989).

26. Discussed in E. Lamirande, "Hypatie, Synesios et la fin des dieux: L'histoire et la fiction," *Studies in Religion (Sciences religieuses)* 18 (1989):467–489.

27. U. Molinaro, "A Christian Martyr in Reverse: Hypatia, 370–415 A.D.," *Hypatia: A Journal of Feminist Philosophy* 4 (1989):6–8.

28. See *Art in America,* April 1980, pp. 115–126; *Art International* 25.7–8 (Sept.–Oct. 1982):52–53. In our day a well-known star of pornographic films adopted Hypatia as her first name.

29. Socrates, *HE* VII.15.

30. *Suda,* s.v. Hypatia (4.645.4–16 Adler) = Dam. frag. 102 (pp. 79.18 and 81.10 Zintzen).

31. Gibbon, *Decline and Fall,* pp. 109–110.

32. Philostorgius, *HE* VIII.9.

33. The letter is in Mansi, *Conciliorum omnium amplissima collectio,* V (Florence, 1751), col. 1007 (*Synodicon,* chap. 216). On the apocryphal nature of the letter see Hoche, pp. 452–453. The letter seems to have originated at the end of antiquity.

34. L. Canfora, *The Vanished Library* (New York, 1990), p. 87.

35. See *PRLE,* I, 657–658. On Palladas also see A. Cameron, "Palladas und Christian Polemic," *Journal of Roman Studies* 55 (1965):17–30.

36. In *AP,* IX, 400 (Stadtmüller).

37. G. Luck, "Palladas Christian or Pagan?" *Harvard Studies in Classical Philology* 63 (1958):455–471.

38. *Suda,* s.v. Panolbios (4.21 Adler); *PRLE,* II, 829; A. Cameron, "Wandering Poets: A Literary Movement in Byzantine Egypt," *Historia* 14 (1965):470–509.

39. *PRLE,* II, 401–402 and 576 (Hypatia 3).

40. Meyer, p. 52.

41. C. Baronius, *Annales Ecclesiatici* (12 vols., 1597–1609), VII (Paris, 1816), p. 56 (46–47).

42. G. Arnolds, *Kirchen und Ketzer-Historie,* I (Frankfurt, 1699), pp. 229–230.

43. S. Le Nain de Tillemont, *Mémoires pour servir à l'histoire écclesiastique des six premiers siècles* (Paris, 1701–1730), XIV, 274–276.

44. J. A. Fabricius, *Bibliotheca Graeca,* VIII (Hamburg, 1717), pp. 219–221; IX (Hamburg, 1719), pp. 718–719; also Aegidius Menagius, *Historia mulierum philosopharum* (Amsterdam, 1692), p. 28. At the end of the seventeenth century the priest and historian C. Fleury included Hypatia in his *Histoire écclesiastique,* V, 23, 25 (Paris, 1697), 434–435.

45. D. J. A. Schmid, *De Hipparcho, duobus Theonibus doctaque Hypatia* (Jena, 1689).

46. J. C. Wernsdorff, "De Hypatia philosopha Alexandrina," in *Dissertationes,* IV: *De Cyrillo episcopo in causa tumultus alexandrini caedisque Hypatiae contra Gothofredum Arnoldum et Joannem Tolandum defenso* (Wittemberg, 1747–48).

47. A. W. Richeson, "Humanismus and History of Mathematics,"

ed. G. W. Dunnington, *National Mathematics Magazine* 15 (1940):74–82.

48. R. Jacobacci, "Women of Mathematics," *Arithmetic Teacher* 17.4 (April 1970):316–324.

49. M. Alic, *Hypatia's Heritage* (Boston, 1986), p. 41. Also introduced into the history of mathematics as a distinguished mathematician by T. Perl, *Math Equals: Biography of Women Mathematicians and Related Activities* (Menlo Park, Calif., 1978), pp. 13–28; M. E. Waithe, ed., *A History of Women Philosophers* (The Hague, 1987), pp. 169–195, uncritically collects old and new views on the erudition and fortunes of Hypatia.

50. B. L. Van der Waerden, *Science Awakening* (New York, 1963), p. 290.

51. M. Bernal, *Black Athena: The Afroasiatic Roots of Classical Civilization* (New Brunswick, N.J., 1987), pp. 121–122.

52. B. Lumpkin, "Hypatia and Women's Rights in Ancient Egypt," in *Black Women in Antiquity, Journal of African Civilization* 6.1 (1984, rev. ed., 1988), pp. 155–156.

II. Hypatia and Her Circle

1. F. Lapatz, *Lettres des Synésius. Traduit pour la première fois et suivies d'études sur les derniers moments de l'Hellénisme* (Paris, 1870), pp. 329–339, and Crawford, pp. 395–405, describe Hypatia's "cenacle" perfunctorily but account for the elements that united her followers. See also C. Bizzochi, "Gl'inni filosofici di Sinesio interpretati come mistiche celebrazioni," *Gregorianum* 33 (1951):350–367; Lacombrade (1951), pp. 47–71; Roques (1989), who traces and describes Synesius' correspondents; and Cameron (1993), chap. 2. Hypatia's students are dealt with in a limited way by Bregman, pp. 20–39. Other discussions of Hypatia and Synesius are Hoche, pp. 436f.; H. Ligier, *De Hypatia philosopha et eclectismi Alexandrini fine* (1879), pp. 19f.; S. Wolf, *Hypatia die Philosophin von Alexandrien* (Vienna, 1879), pp. 22f.; Meyer, pp. 14f.; G. Grützmacher, *Synesius von Kyrene: Ein Charakterbild aus dem Untergang des Hellenentums* (Leipzig, 1913), pp. 23–30; J. C. Pando, *The Life and Times of Synesius of Cyrene as Revealed in His Works* (Washington, D.C., 1940), pp. 72f.

2. Collected in Garzya (1979). The English translations here (with

some modifications) are from A. Fitzgerald, *The Letters of Synesius of Cyrene,* I (Oxford, 1926). On modern philological studies of the letters see A. Garzya, *Storia e interpretazione di testi bizantini: Saggi e ricerche,* Variorum Reprints 28 (London, 1974), chaps. 21–28: Garzya (1979), pp. vii–lxiii. Among the studies devoted to late antiquity that draw on the letters of Synesius are Cameron (1993); A. Cameron, "Earthquake 400," *Chiron* 17 (1987):343–360; and Roques (1987) and (1989), although the last invites controversy regarding its chronology. Roques has also written several articles: "Synésios de Cyrène et les migrations berbères vers l'Orient," *Comptes rendus de l'Académie des inscriptions et belles-lettres,* Nov.–Dec. 1983, pp. 660–677; "Synésios de Cyrène et le Silphion de Cyrènaïque," *REG* 97 (1984):218–231; "L'économie de la Cyrènaïque au Bas-Empire," *British Archaeological Reports,* ser. 236 (1985) = *Cyrenaica in Antiquity* (Cambridge, 1983).

3. Cameron in *Chiron* 17 (1987):355–360 rejects the dating of Synesius' embassy to 399–402 established by O. Seeck, "Studien zu Synesius," *Philologus* 52 (1894):442–483. Roques supports Seeck's view and fixes Synesius' years of study from 390/395 until 398. Also see his "La lettre 4 de Synésios de Cyrène," *REG* 90 (1977):263–295; Lacombrade (1951), pp. 314–315, believes Synesius studied before 395, but he agrees with Seeck on the date of Synesius' departure for Constantinople.

4. Synesius returned to Cyrene via Alexandria, having left Constantinople during the earthquake in 400 (*Ep.* 61). He returned for an extensive stay in Alexandria in the early 400s after a year's sojourn in Cyrene; Cameron in *Chiron* 17 (1987):359.

5. See chronological tables in Roques (1987), p. 451, and (1989), p. 247. Lacombrade (1951), pp. 131–138, sees Synesius in Alexandria in 402 and later in 403–404. The dating of his ascendance to the bishopric of Ptolemais is particularly controversial in the literature. See, for instance, T. D. Barnes, "When Did Synesius Become Bishop of Ptolemais?" *GRBS* 27.3 (1986):325–329.

6. *PRLE,* II, 545.

7. H. Druon, *Etudes sur la vie et les oeuvres de Synésios, évêque de Ptolémais* (Paris, 1859), p. 272, thought he came, like Synesius, from Cyrene; Lacombrade (1951), p. 53, is inclined to accept Egypt as his homeland; Roques (1989), p. 87 n. 2, believes he was a Syrian.

8. On the study fees see A. Müller, "Studentenleben im 4 Jahrhundert n. Chr.," *Philologus,* n.s. 23 (1910):292–317; and H. I. Marrou, *Histoire de l'éducation dans l'antiquité,* 6th ed. (Paris, 1965), pp. 305–306.

9. They are quoted extensively in *Ad Paeonium de dono* 5 (p. 550 G); *AG,* App., VI, 74 (Cougny).

10. *AP,* IX, 577. See Neugebauer (1975), II, 335–336 and n. 22; earlier Lacombrade (1951), pp. 56–57. In *Ep.* 141 Synesius also mentions iambic poems that he has sent to his friend, asking him to return them. These, too, are probably not his poems but those of another author whom Synesius liked and copied.

11. *PRLE,* II, 336 (Cyrus 1 and 7). On Cyrus of Panopolis see Chuvin, pp. 93–94, 122. I agree with Haas, p. 256. Although the name Cyrus was common during the period, in this case we are dealing with a narrow circle of the intellectual elite.

12. See Cameron in *Historia* 14 (1965):470–509; G. W. Bowersock, *Hellenism in Late Antiquity* (Ann Arbor, 1990), pp. 4, 43.

13. *PRLE,* II, 816–817 (Paeonius 1); ibid., 1013–1014 (Simplicius 2). On that *comes,* who is usually identified as Paeonius, see, for example, Fitzgerald, *Letters of Synesius,* I, p. 186; Lacombrade (1951), p. 123; Roques (1987), pp. 221–222, 227–228, and (1989), pp. 75–84, 93–94; Garzya (1989), p. 354; Cameron (1993), pp. 84–91. Roques points to Simplicius, *comes et magister utriusque militiae per Orientem,* who in 398–399 was reorganizing the military command in Libya and established the post dux Libyarum. Cameron has collected and sorted out the discussions published so far on that "comes."

14. *PRLE,* II, 800–801 (Olympius 1); Roques (1989), pp. 105–115. In this letter (*Ep.* 140) Synesius describes Olympius as a devotee of horses and arrows.

15. Provided we accept the dating of the letter as proposed by Garzya (1979), p. 163, and Roques (1987), p. 452.

16. *PRLE,* II, 1111; on the descent of Theotimus of Cyrene see D. T. Runia, "Another Wandering Poet," *Historia* 28 (1979):254–256; Cameron in *Historia* 14 (1965):476–477, 505.

17. *PRLE,* II, 553 (Hesychius 5); Lacombrade (1951), pp. 50–51; Roques (1987), pp. 166, 206–212, 322–333, maintains that Hesychius was not only a member of the *curiales* in Cyrene but also acted as *defensor civitatis* from 407 (or 412) and was a Libyarch—that is, the chief priest

of the province Pentapolis—around 400. In addition he asserts that the beautiful, luxurious house ornamented with Christian mosaics, uncovered in the center of Cyrene during archaeological excavations, belonged to this Hesychius, Synesius' companion. Cameron (1993), pp. 17–18, is doubtful about Hesychius' connections with Cyrene, and believes that this house was the property of the family of Synesius' father, whose name was also Hesychius.

18. *PRLE,* II, 442; Euoptius' letters are analyzed by Roques (1989), pp. 161–196.

19. That Euoptius began studying in Alexandria later than Synesius is evidenced in *Ep.* 53, in which Synesius describes to his brother his first voyage to Alexandria, probably for study, in the 390s. See also Lacombrade (1951), p. 54 and n. 49.

20. See Garzya (1989), p. 238 n. 5. We are reminded here of Pythagoras' opinion that friends share everything, that friendship means equality (D.L. VIII.1.10). He repeats the example mentioned in *Ep.* 93 in *Ep.* 131 to Pylaemenes, a friend from Constantinople.

21. *PRLE,* II, 422, and Roques (1987), pp. 340 and 363.

22. In this letter Synesius uses the term *to syntrophos,* which means "childhood playmate" (see L.S.J.). Fitzgerald, *Letters of Synesius,* I, p. 109, translates the term as "our old housemate"; Garzya (1989), p. 159, renders it as "nostro vecchio compagno."

23. *PRLE,* I, 908 (perhaps Theotecnus 3?).

24. *PRLE,* II, 176. Fragments of his writings were collected by H. Rabe, "Aus Rhetoren Handschriften," *Rheinisches Museum für Philologie* 62 (1907):586–590.

25. *PRLE,* II, 1099 (Theodosius 3). Compare also R. A. Koster, *Guardians of Language: The Grammarian and Society in Late Antiquity* (Berkeley, 1988), p. 366.

26. Garzya (1979), p. 289; Roques (1989), pp. 230–231, contends that nothing else can be said about this individual.

27. Dam. frag. 102 (p. 79.14–15 Zintzen).

28. *PRLE,* II, 810–811 (Orestes 1).

29. *HE* VII.15.

30. Ibid., 14.

31. *Chron.* 84.87–88 (p. 100 Charles). Zintzen, p. 79.14, asserts that the term *archontes* refers to Orestes, the prefect of Egypt. Haas, p. 256,

reads Damascius' sentence thus: "It was even customary for newly elected magistrates to pay her a courtesy visit upon taking up their office"; Rougé (1990), p. 499, thinks, after Socrates, that this fragment refers instead to frequent routine meetings with clerks.

32. Rist, p. 216 and n. 12.

33. See note 13. Paeonius, whom Synesius met in Constantinople (*Ep.* 154), was another such *comes.*

34. *PRLE,* II, 858 (Pentadius 1); Roques (1989), pp. 223–224.

35. *PRLE,* II, 531 (Heliodorus 2); Garzya (1979), p. 291.

36. Roques (1987), p. 171, and (1989), p. 227.

37. The neutrality of the Alexandrian school was stressed by K. Praechter in F. Überweg, *Grundriss der Geschichte der Philosophie,* I, ed. K. Praechter (Basel, 1953), p. 635. The tradition of tolerance was maintained until the time of Aeneas of Gaza and John Philoponus. See, among others, H. I. Marrou, "Synesius of Cyrene and Alexandrian Neoplatonism," in *The Conflict between Paganism and Christianity in the Fourth Century* (Oxford, 1963), p. 140; R. T. Wallis, *Neoplatonism* (London, 1972), p. 139; Haas, p. 226f.

38. On Isidore of Pelusium see A. Bouvy, *De S. Isidoro Pelosiota libri tres* (Nîmes, 1884), pp. 11f.; L. Bayer, *Isidors von Pelusium* (Paderborn, 1915); P. Evieux, "Isidore de Péluse," *Recherches de Sciences religieuses* 64.3 (1976):321–340.

39. Crawford, pp. 415, 515–516, where we find also the translation of Isidore's four letters. These are *Epp.* I, 232, 241, 418, 483 = *PG* 78, 330C, 350B, 416B, 446B. *Ep.* 241 concerns Arians and Eunomians, that is, the same topic Synesius touched on in *Ep.* 44 to Olympius. Evieux ("Isidore de Péluse," p. 326) points out that another of Isidore's correspondents is Olympius, who may be Synesius' friend of that name.

40. Lacombrade (1951), pp. 54–55, 63.

41. Garzya (1989), pp. 347 n. 5, 350 n. 3, 564 n. 27, 568 n. 53. Roques (1987), p. 303, is unable to identify the later St. Isidore among Hypatia's students.

42. Crawford, p. 582 (index), compares similar fragments that occur in both collections; pp. 185–186 are particularly interesting. Bregman, p. 24 and n. 26, echoes Crawford's and Lacombrade's opinion. Lacombrade's view is cautiously shared by Marrou, "Synesius of Cyrene and Alexandrian Platonism," p. 140.

43. G. Redl, "Isidor von Pelusium," *Zeitschrift für Kirchengeschichte* 47.2 (1928):325–332.

44. *Ep.* II, 215 = *PG* 78, 656–657.

45. *Chron.* 84.88 (p. 101 Charles).

46. In the light of these findings, the anecdote related by John Moschos in his *Pratum Spirituale* (208–209 Maisonno) arouses some surprise. He recounts that during his stay in Alexandria he heard a story about Synesius' having converted the philosopher Evagrius, his former fellow student. Synesius supposedly met him in Cyrene when he was already bishop; see Fowden (1979), p. 189, who regards this story as sheer fiction.

47. Cameron (1993), pp. 15–41, strongly emphasizes that Synesius was a Christian by birth and never ceased being one. Roques is of the same opinion. Lacombrade (1951), pp. 63, 274–275; Marrou, "La 'conversion' de Synésios," *REG* 65 (1952):474–484; and Bregman, pp. 19, 39, disagree. They set Synesius' "conversion" at the earliest in the period of his diplomatic mission to Constantinople. In their opinion he was possessed of a deeply anchored religious inclination that until his ascension to the bishopric was gradually evolving into full Christianity.

48. *PRLE,* II, 1049; and Lacombrade (1951), pp. 210–212, date the consecration to 411, as does J. H. W. G. Liebeschüetz, *Barbarians and Bishops: Army, Church and State in the Age of Arcadius and Chrysostom* (Oxford, 1990), p. 232. As already mentioned, Barnes, in *GRBS* 27.3 (1986), accepts 407, a surprisingly early date. Roques (1987), pp. 301–317, argues that Synesius was baptized during a visit in Alexandria (Easter 404) and was elected bishop on January 1, 412. Cameron (1993), p. 21 and n. 35, contends that he became bishop of Ptolemais in 410. Liebeschüetz surveys the discussion of the issue until 1986, "Why Did Synesius Become Bishop of Ptolemais?" *Byzantion* 56 (1986):180–195. On Synesius' baptism see Cameron (1993), pp. 29–37.

49. For example, E. R. Hardy, *Christian Egypt: Church and People, Christianity, and Nationalism in the Patriarchate of Alexandria* (New York and Oxford, 1952), pp. 85ff. Rougé (1990), p. 487, evaluates Theophilus' conduct less critically.

50. "The divine Plato in particular exercised what almost amounted

to an intellectual monopoly in late antiquity. However his doctrines might be interpreted, *the authority of his name was absolute,*" writes Fowden, the best specialist on philosophical circles of late antiquity; "The Platonist Philosopher and His Circle in Late Antiquity," *Philosophia* 7 (1977):360–361.

51. The philosopher's divinity constitutes a basic element in the biographies of Late Platonic philosophers. They all are "divine men," for only a "holy man" may be a philosopher now. For this reason philosophers of this period, besides Plotinus and Porphyry, were referred to as priests. See P. Athanassiadi-Fowden, *Julian and Hellenism: An Intellectual Biography* (Oxford, 1981), pp. 181–182; G. Fowden, "The Pagan Holy Man in Late Antique Society," *JHS* 102 (1982):34–37 and n. 33. Fowden (1979), passim, discusses the type of the philosopher-priest in the fourth century. Just as Synesius calls Hypatia *theios* (holy) or *theiotatos* (holiest), so does the emperor Julian call Iamblichus and Pythagoras: for instance, *Julian, Epistulae, Leges, Poemata, Fragmenta,* ed. J. Bidez and F. Cumont (Paris, 1922), p. 12 (*Ep.* 4), p. 15.14, where Iamblichus is called by the same name as Plato and Pythagoras, and 98 (*Ep.* 27), p. 158.18. Eunapius defines Sosipatra with like terms in *VS* VI.9.3, 8. Cameron (1993), pp. 51–52, assumes that Eunapius could have had Hypatia in mind when describing Sosipatra. He follows Penella's suggestion, pp. 61–62.

52. In the sources the term "guide" *(kathegetes)* is accorded to philosophers such as Porphyry, Iamblichus, Themistius, and Damascius. The explanation of its meaning can be found in Athanassiadi-Fowden, *Julian and Hellenism,* p. 34 and n. 96. The emperor Julian bestowed the appellation on his preceptor Maximus of Ephesus (ibid., p. 185). Rist, pp. 218–219 and n. 22, writes that Hierocles, the first important Neoplatonic Alexandrian philosopher of the fifth century, called his master Plutarch *kathegetes.*

53. Origen III (p. 35 Foerster). The term *choros* describing a master's disciples was quite common in the fourth and fifth centuries. See Fowden (1979), p. 79. For example, in *Vita Isidori* (Dam. frag. 124, p. 107 Zintzen) Athenian philosophers admiring Aedesia's accomplishments are called *choros ton philosophon,* and their leader *ho koryphaios Proklos.*

54. On this Platonic metaphor see Lacombrade (1951), p. 60; and

Bregman, p. 26 n. 32. Both Lacombrade (47–63) and Bregman (24–29) attempt to reconstruct Hypatia's teachings generally (Bregman somewhat better than Lacombrade).

55. Porphyry, *Vita Plotini* 2.25–27; on this topic see Bregman, p. 26.

56. On the use of this term by Synesius see Bizzochi in *Gregorianum* 33 (1951):358–362. This is a general concept commonly used to elucidate the theurgical elevation in the Chaldean Oracles; H. Lewy, *The Chaldean Oracles and Theurgy* (Paris, 1978), pp. 177–226, 487–489. Synesius also applies the variant form *agoge* (*Dion* 9).

57. All Neoplatonists strive toward the ultimate goal of philosophizing. Fowden (1979), p. 11, defines Plotinus' philosophical course as "a clear vision of the One." See *Enneads* I.6 and 7.

58. Dam. frag. 102 (p. 77.15–17 Zintzen).

59. Ibid., lines 11–13 Zintzen.

60. Cameron (1993), p. 44. In this view Hypatia reveals herself rather as a Pythagorean, regarding music in combination with mathematics as a salutary means to the soul's harmony. Compare W. K. C. Guthrie, *A History of Greek Philosophy*, I (Cambridge, 1962), pp. 306ff. In *De musica* (1145B) Plutarch discusses the great importance Pythagoras assigned to music and its rationalizing effect. Compare on this topic Dam., *Epit. Phot.* 127 and notes (p. 170 Zintzen); also Garzya (1989), p. 710 n. 103.

61. For example, this is what D. Shanzer does, citing similar instances of the conduct of women professing Cynic philosophy (though never to this extreme degree); "Merely a Cynic Gesture," *Rivista di filologia e istruzione classica* 113 (1985):61–66. Similar examples have been also collected by Asmus in *Studien zur verleichenden Literaturgeschichte* 7 (1907):15–16; G. Bigoni, "Ipazia Alessandrina," *Atti del' Instituto Veneto di scienze, lettere ed arti* 5, ser. 6 (1886–87):505–506; Lacombrade (1951), p. 45 and n. 42; Cameron (1993), pp. 43–44, 60–61. Sosipatra also drives away suitors: Eunapius, *VS* VI.9.3–13.

62. Socrates, repudiating Alcibiades, declares that he must discover in him invisible beauty, "and if on espying this you are trying for a mutual exchange of beauty for beauty it is no slight advantage you are counting on—you are trying to get genuine in return for reputed beauties and in fact are designing to fetch off the old bargain of gold for bronze!" And he adds, "Remember, the intellectual sight begins

to be keen when visual is entering on its wane; but you are a long way yet from that time"; *Symposium* 218E.

63. Plotinus, *Enneads* I.6.8.

64. Dam. frag. 102 (p. 77.7–8 Zintzen). This is in keeping with the division/classification in *Nicomachean Ethics* (1103a6–7) that assigns sophrosyne to virtues connected with active, political life (compare H. North, *Sophrosyne: Self-Knowledge and Self-Restraint in Greek Literature* [Ithaca, 1965], pp. 200–205).

65. On the concept of sophrosyne in late Greek philosophy see North, *Sophrosyne,* pp. 231–257; in Byzantine literature, R. Elwin Lindahl, Jr., "A Study of Sophrosyne in Non-Theological Byzantine Literature" (Ph.D. diss., Tulane University, 1971).

66. Cassiodorus, *Hist. Eccl. Trip.* XI.12; Nicephorus Callistus, *Eccl. Hist.* XIV.16.469–470.

67. See Garzya (1989), pp. 340 n. 4 and 341 n. 6. Synesius is here concerned with the canon of cardinal virtues and their development together with the process of the soul's ascent. Synesius makes use of the classification of cardinal virtues introduced by Porphyry (*Sententiae* 32, pp. 22–35 Lamberz); North, *Sophrosyne,* pp. 239–240, demonstrates the Neoplatonist's various definitions and designations of the stages.

68. Hypatia's virginity brings her closer to the saintly Christian woman than to the pagan ones, who usually married. On Greek, Roman, and Christian virginity see Peter Brown, *The Body and Society: Men, Women, and Sexual Renunciation in Early Christianity* (Boston, 1988), pp. 8–9, 260–263, 276–277. This problem is also discussed in numerous studies of women, for example, E. Clark, *Ascetic Piety and Women's Faith* (Lewiston, 1986). On the Neoplatonic idea of sophrosyne together with *katharotes* (chastity) and *hagneia* (holiness) see North, *Sophrosyne,* pp. 30–31, 236–242. See also Hazel E. Barnes, "Katharsis in the Enneads of Plotinus," *Transactions and Proceedings of the American Philological Association* 73 (1942):358–382.

69. *Ad Paeonium* 4 (p. 544 Garzya).

70. *Suda,* s.v. Hypatia, there cited, reconstructed on the basis of Hesychius. See Chapter III.

71. Fowden in *Philosophia* 7 (1977):380–382; just as all known philosophers were teaching mathematics (Cameron [1991], p. 87 n. 200);

on the renaissance of Pythagorean philosophy and mathematics see D. O'Meara, *Pythagoras Revived: Mathematics and Philosophy in Late Antiquity* (Oxford, 1989).

72. Dam., *Epit. Phot.* 164 (p. 218 Zintzen).

73. In general not much is known about fourth-century philosophy in Alexandria. On this topic see Fowden (1979), pp. 301–304. On the two other philosophers, Hypatia's contemporaries Olympius and Antoninus, see Chapter III. On Alexandrian Neoplatonism see I. Hadot, *Le problème du Néoplatonisme Alexandrin: Hieroclés et Simplicius* (Paris, 1978); and N. Aujoulat, *Le Néoplatonisme Alexandrin* (Leiden, 1986).

74. Compare Fowden in *Philosophia* 7 (1977):359.

75. Meyer, p. v; Hoche, p. 442; Lacombrade (1951), p. 44 and n. 37; Marrou, "Synesius of Cyrene and Alexandrian Neoplatonism," p. 134; Rist, p. 210; E. Evrard in *REG* 90 (1977):69–74; Haas, p. 276 n. 169.

76. See, among others, Evrard in *REG* 90 (1977):71–72; Chuvin, p. 86. Cameron collects the discussion on the topic (1993), pp. 43–45. The argument has been supported by a story about a young student in love with Hypatia; the story is sometimes given a Cynic character (Shanzer, "Merely a Cynic Gesture," pp. 62f.).

77. Cameron (1993), pp. 27–28, 56–57, 63ff. On the tribon, or philosophical mantle, see LSJ. It was worn by Socrates, the Spartans, the Stoics, the Cynics, and in the circle of Ammonius Saccas (Fowden in *Philosophia* 7 [1977]:369).

78. Haas, p. 226, mentions such lecture halls excavated in Kom-el-Dikka.

79. Penella, p. 48 n. 24.

80. Compare Garzya (1979), p. 348 n. 7. On the importance of the Pythagorean *tetractys* see Guthrie, *History of Greek Philosophy,* pp. 213, 225; O'Meara, *Pythagorus Revived,* p. 17; and Lacombrade (1951), p. 47.

81. Plotinus, *Enneads* VI.9–11. In *Vita Plotini* 3 Porphyry relates that Plotinus and his companion Herennius and Orygenes the pagan decided to keep secret the philosophy that Ammonius told them, but they broke their resolve.

82. Philostratus, *Vita Apollonii* I, 1.

83. Hypatia turns again to a Platonic expression (compare *Republic* I, 343C).

84. On the criticism of philosophers and monks in *Dion* see Cameron (1993), pp. 62–69; A. Garzya, "Il Dione de Sinesio nel quadro del dibattito culturale del IV secolo," *Rivista di filologia e istruzione classica* 100 (1972):32–45; R. Lizzi, "Ascetismo e predicanzione urbana nell'Egitto del V secolo," *Atti dell'Istituto Veneto di scienze, lettere ed arti* 141 (1982–83):139–145.

85. Cameron (1993), pp. 50–51, compiles all existing discussions on the topic as well as those on the so-called Alexandrian school. Fowden is of like opinion in *Classical Philology* 80 (1985):283–284 (review of Bregman's book on Synesius) and in *The Egyptian Hermes: A Historical Approach to the Late Pagan Mind* (Cambridge, 1986), pp. 179–182.

86. Ibid., p. 51; on Antoninus see Chapter III.

87. *Vita Procli* 28 (p. 84 Masullo).

88. My assertion is based on an IBYCUS computer search of the text, which I carried out at the Center for Hellenic Studies in Washington with the kind assistance of Zeph Stewart, then director of the Center. Terms such as *kathegemon, choros, orgia,* and *anagoge* recur from Porphyry to Marinus. The attributes, conduct, and ethos of the "divine man" in Neoplatonic biographies have been collected and analyzed by P. Cox, *Biography in Late Antiquity: A Quest for the Holy Man* (Berkeley, 1983); also S. L. Karren, "Near Eastern Culture and Hellenic Paideia in Damascius' Life of Isidore" (Ph.D. diss., University of Wisconsin, 1978).

89. On what was read in Neoplatonic circles see M.-O. Goulet-Cazé, "L'arrière—plan scolaire de la Vie de Plotin," in *Porphyre, La Vie de Plotin,* I (Paris, 1982), pp. 259–273.

90. The dependence of Synesius' philosophy on dogmas and views in the Chaldean Oracles is analyzed by W. Theiler, *Die chaldaischen Orakel und die Hymnen des Synesios* (Halle, 1942); U. von Wilamowitz Moellendorf, *Die Hymnen des Proklos und Synesios, SPAW.PH* 1907/I, 271–295 = *Kleine Schriften* (Berlin, 1941), II, 163–191; E. des Places, ed., *Oracles Chaldaiques* (Paris, 1971), pp. 31–41; Lewy, *The Chaldean Oracles,* pp. 118, 161f., 203 and n. 114, 343f., 358, 476; S. Vollenweider, *Neuplatonische und christliche Theologie bei Synesios von Kyrene*

(Göttingen, 1985), pp. 14, 50f., 105ff., 189ff. On references to the Chaldean Oracles in *De insomniis* see R. V. Kissling, "The Oxhema-Pneuma of the Neoplatonists and the De Insomniis of Synesius of Cyrene," *American Journal of Philology* 43 (1922):318–330.

91. The popularity of Platonic texts in Egypt in Hypatia's time is evinced in their presence in Gnostic literature from the library discovered at Nag Hammadi; L. Painchaud, "Fragment de la République de Platon," in *Bibliothèque Copte de Nag Hammadi,* Section "Textes" 11 (Quebec, 1983), pp. 109–161. See also O. Montevecchi, *La papirologia* (Rome, 1973), p. 354.

92. On Hermeticism in Synesius compare Bizzochi in *Gregorianum* 33 (1951):368–381. Synesius' connections with Hermeticism are pointed out by Fowden in *Classical Philology* 80 (1985):283–284 and *The Egyptian Hermes,* p. 179; and Cameron (1993), pp. 52–53.

93. Cameron (1993), chap. VII, 5 and 6.

94. Ibid., p. 107.

95. On Iamblichus' school and theurgic method of philosophy see P. Boyancè, "Theurgie et télestique néoplatoniciennes," *Revue de l'histoire des religions* 147 (1955):189–209; L. W. Leadbeater, "Aspects of the Philosophical Priesthood in Iamblichus 'De Mysteriis,' " *Classical Bulletin* 47 (1970):89–92; des Places, ed., *Oracles Chaldaiques,* pp. 12–18; E. des Places, "La religion de Jamblique," in *Jamblique à Proclus,* Entretiens sur l'Antiquité Classique XXI (1974), pp. 78–94; Lewy, *The Chaldean Oracles,* pp. 27–57, 259–309; Athanassiadi-Fowden, *Julian and Hellenism,* pp. 31ff.

96. Bizzochi in *Gregorianum* 33 (1951).

97. C. Lacombrade, ed. and trans., *Synésios de Cyrène, Hymnes* (Paris, 1978), pp. 77–78, 98–99. For an analysis of *Hymn* IX see Bregman, pp. 29–40, concluding his examination of Synesius' studies with Hypatia.

98. Compare Cameron (1993), pp. 30ff.

99. Eusebius of Caesarea, *Praeparatio Evangelica* IV.13; M. Dzielska, *Apollonius of Tyana in Legend and History* (Rome, 1986), pp. 138, 140.

100. See Fowden in *Philosophia* 7 (1977); and (1979). For information on Iamblichean philosophical circles of late Hellenism see Penella.

III. The Life and Death of Hypatia

1. This is how Dam. frag. 102 (p. 79.14–15 Zintzen) has been interpreted. See, for example, H. Druon, *Etudes sur la vie et les oeuvres de Synésios, évêque de Ptolémais* (Paris, 1859), p. 10; Bigoni in *Atti del'Instituto Veneto di scienze, lettere ed arti* 5, ser. 6 (1886–87):502–503.

2. Haas is the most useful monograph on the Alexandria of Hypatia. It includes a comprehensive bibliography on the history of the city (pp. 327–353). On the architecture of the late Roman part of Alexandria see M. Rodziewicz, *Les habitations romaines tardives d'Alexandrie à la lumière des fouillies polonaise à Kom-el-Dikka,* III (Warsaw, 1984).

3. The proclivity of the city's inhabitants to rowdiness has been discussed by both ancient and contemporary authors. Thus for Durrell, Alexandria is always an abyss of contradiction: "Alexandria princess and whore. The royal city and the anus mundi"; *Clea* (1986), p. 700. Elsewhere he writes: "One must try to reconcile two extremes of habit and behavior which are not due to the intellectual disposition of the inhabitants, but to their soil, air, landscape. I mean extreme sensuality and intellectual asceticism"; *Justine* (1986), p. 83.

4. See Hoche, p. 440 and n. 22; Meyer, p. 8.

5. Thus Hypateia appears as a name in papyrus in F. Preisigke, *Namenbuch* (Heidelberg, 1922), col. 451, entry; on another papyrus, however, the name appears more frequently as Hypatia, in D. Foraboschi, *Onomasticon Alterum Papyrologicum,* Supp. al. Namenbuch di F. Preisigke (Milan, 1971), p. 325 = Testi e Documenti per lo Studio dell'Antichità 16, seria papirologica 2. The name also appears in inscriptions; see V. Langlois, *Inscriptions grecques romaines, byzantines et arméniennes de la Cilicie* (Paris, 1854), p. 11, no. 24. Hypatia was a traditional name in the family of St. Philaret of Paphlagonia; M.-H. Fourmy and M. Leroy, "La vie de S. Philarète," *Byzantion* 9.1 (1934):140. A Hypatia founded a convent in Constantinople; *La géographie ecclésiastique de l'empire Byzantine,* I.3: *Les églises et les monastères,* ed. R. Jauin (Paris, 1953), p. 506. This may have been the saintly donor Hypatia (discussed in the Sources) or Hypatia (2) of *PRLE* II, p. 576. In Pseudo-Zacharias' *Historia Ecclesiastica* we also read about another saintly Hypatia (formerly a pagan) in Syria (in Camuliana) who in the sixth century founded a church in veneration of Christ's miraculous

picture; Pseudo-Zacharias, *Historia Ecclesiastica,* ed. E. W. Brooks, pt. II, p. 199, 1.6.

6. *Byzantina Historia* 8.3 (I, 294 Bonn).

7. Ἐπιτάφιοι λόγοι A. 85. Μεσαιωνικὴ βιβλιοθήκη 5, 59, ed. K. N. Sathas (Paris, 1876). Nicephorus Gregoras undoubtedly imitated Psellus. (Compare K. Krumbacher, *Geschichte der byzantinischen Literature* [Munich, 1897²], p. 504.)

8. Hoche, p. 439; Meyer, p. 9; K. Praechter in *RE* (1914), col. 242; Rist, p. 215; Evrard in *REG* 90 (1977):69; V. Lambropoulou in *Hypatia* 1 (1984): 4; and others. Today Cameron (1993), p. 52, also inclines to the traditional date.

9. *Suda,* s.v. Hypatia (4.644.3 Adler) = Hesychius, *Onomatologus* (p. 219 Flach).

10. *Chronogr.* XIV.

11. S. Wolf, *Hypatia die Philosophin von Alexandrien* (Vienna, 1879), p. 12. This view is shared by R. Volkmann, *Synesius von Cyrene* (Berlin, 1869), p. 252; A. Gardner, *Synesius of Cyrene, Philosopher and Bishop* (London, 1886); in the popular article by J. McCabe in *The Critic* 43 (1903), who gives her fifty-five years at the time of her death; and Lacombrade (1951), p. 39.

12. Penella, pp. 126–129. Philostorgius (*HE* VIII.9; p. 11 Bidez), who places Hypatia's life during the reigns of Valentinian and Valens, probably has in mind her studies with Theon. This argument supports my supposition that she was born before 370.

13. Roques (1989), pp. 21–36, has surveyed all the discussions on the date of Synesius' birth.

14. Cameron (1993), p. 15 and n. 1.

15. *Suda,* s.v. Theon (2.702.9–15 Adler).

16. *Chronogr.* XIII (p. 343 Bonn).

17. Compare A. Tihon, *Le "Petit Commentaire" de Théon d'Alexandrie aux tables faciles de Ptolemée* (Vatican, 1978), p. 1 n. 3; G. J. Toomer, *Ptolemy's Almagest* (London, 1984), pp. 652–655.

18. For example, Fowden (1979), p. 179, establishes the dates of Theon's life for 300/40–400.

19. *Suda,* s.vv. Pappos (4.26.4 Adler) and Theon; also *PRLE,* I, 667.

20. On Pappus' and Theon's collaboration in the context of the chronology of their life see A. Rome, *Commentaires de Pappus et de*

Théon d'Alexandrie sur l'Almagest, 3 vols. (Vatican, 1931–1943; reprint, 1967), I, v–xx; Neugebauer (1975), I, 5 and II, 965–966; Toomer, *Ptolemy's Almagest,* p. 2.

21. All scholars point out that Theon was the last member of the Museion. Compare Lacombrade in *Bulletin de la Societé Toulousaine d'études classiques* 166 (1972):10; Fowden (1979), p. 190 n. 5; N. G. Wilson, *Scholars of Byzantium* (London, 1983), p. 42; *Oxford Dictionary of Byzantium* (1991).

22. After Aristotle mathematics was considered part of theoretical philosophy. See J. L. Heiberg, *Geschichte der Mathematik und Naturwissenschaften in Altertum* (Munich, 1925), pp. 60f.; H. Hunger, *Die hochsprachliche profane Literatur der Byzantiner* (Munich, 1978), pp. 222–229; Fowden (1979), pp. 63–64, 179; Toomer, *Ptolemy's Almagest,* p. 35; I. Hadot, *Arts libéraux et philosophies dans la pensée antique* (Paris, 1984), pp. 216 n. 3, 252–261. A. Wadberg best demonstrates the connection between mathematics and philosophy in antiquity; *A History of Philosophy,* I: *Antiquity and the Middle Ages* (Oxford, 1982).

23. Socrates, *HE* VII.15; Hesychius in *Suda,* s.v. Hypatia 4 (644.1–2 Adler); Theophanes, *Chronogr.* I (p. 82.16 Bonn); Malalas, *Chronogr.* XIII (p. 343.10 Bonn). The Alexandrian Theon has been also mistaken for Theon of Smyrna, a philosopher of the beginning of the second century who combined Platonic studies with mathematics; J. Dillon, *The Middle Platonists, 80 B.C. to A.D. 220* (New York, 1977), pp. 397–399; Neugebauer (1975), II, 949–950.

24. Compare *CCAG* 5[3], pp. 50.20 (frag. 177 Heeg), 127.11–16 (frag. 171 Heeg), 128.15–18.

25. For Theon's works see *Thesaurus Linguae Graecae: Canon of Greek Authors and Works,* 2d ed. (New York and Oxford, 1986), 311/2033; also K. Ziegler, "Theon 15," *RE* V, A.2 (1934), pp. 2078–79; G. J. Toomer, *Dictionary of Scientific Biography,* XIII (1976), p. 322; *Oxford Dictionary of Byzantium* (1991).

26. *Elements,* in *Euclidis Opera Omnia,* ed. J. L. Heiberg et al., V (Leipzig, 1896), pp. xxxii–xlix; *Optics, Catoptrics,* VII (Leipzig, 1895), pp. xlix–l (it is claimed that Theon was also the editor of Pseudo-Euclid's *Catoptrics,* or *Mirrors*). On Theon's editions of Euclid also Heiberg, *Geschichte der Mathematik,* pp. 15–16, 20f., 44, 75, 78; Neugebauer (1975), II, 893; Tihon (1978), 1; Cameron (1993), pp. 45–50.

27. Rome, *Commentaires de Pappus et de Théon,* I, vff.; Neugebauer (1975), II, 838 nn. 16 and 17.

28. Compare Mogenet (1985); Tihon (1978).

29. Mogenet (1985), pp. 70, 213.

30. Rome, *Commentaires de Pappus et de Théon,* II, 317; Tihon (1978), p. 199; Mogenet (1985), p. 218 and n. 15.

31. Even today Mogenet (1985), p. 218, is not sure whether to regard him as a student or a son of Theon's.

32. For example, in eastern pseudoepigraphs, see Dzielska, *Apollonius of Tyana,* pp. 113–115. This form was used interchangeably with *pais;* see LSJ, s.v. *teknon.* Already in Homer an older person addresses a younger one as *phile teknon.* The astrologer Paulus of Alexandria, dedicating his handbook on astronomy to the student Cronammon, addresses him as *o phile pai kronommon* and then states that *pais* has edited the work with him; J. A. Fabricius, *Bibliotheca Graeca,* IV (Hamburg, 1745), p. 139.

33. Rome, *Commentaires de Pappus et de Théon,* III, 807.

34. On the reception of Theon's writings see J. Lippert, *Studien auf dem Gebiete der griechisch-arabischen Übersetzungsliteratur* (Braunschweig, 1894), pp. 539f.; Neugebauer (1975), I, 838; *Oxford Dictionary of Byzantium,* s.v. Theon.

35. *Suda,* s.v. Hypatia (4.644.4–5 Adler).

36. T. Perl, *Math Equals: Biography of Women Mathematicians and Related Activities* (Menlo Park, Calif., 1978), pp. 13–26. On Apollonius of Perge see Neugebauer (1975), II, 262–273; Cameron (1993), pp. 49–50.

37. See, for example, T. L. Heath, *Diophantus of Alexandria: A Study in the History of Greek Algebra* (New York, 1964), pp. 5, 15, 18. For recent studies of the question see Cameron (1993), p. 49.

38. Cameron (1993).

39. Rome, *Commentaires de Pappus et de Théon,* III, 807; on Hypatia's work on *Almagest* see pp. cxvi–cxxi; Mogenet (1985), p. 69; this view was advanced much earlier by J. F. Montucla, *Histoire des mathématiques,* I (Paris, 1799), p. 332.

40. Cameron (1993), pp. 46–49; also Toomer, *Ptolemy's Almagest,* pp. 5, 683.

41. Cameron (1993), p. 48.

42. Philostorgius, p. 111 Bidez.

43. *Suda,* s.v. Theon.

44. On Theon's astrolabe see O. Neugebauer, "The Early History of the Astrolabe," *Isis* 40 (1949):240; Neugebauer (1975), II, 873, 877–878; Cameron (1993), pp. 54–55.

45. Neugebauer (1975), II, 873.

46. Cameron (1993), p. 55, believes Theon was no longer alive when Synesius was studying with Hypatia.

47. *Chronogr.* XIII (p. 343 Bonn).

48. Suda, s.v. Theon (2.702.13–14 Adler).

49. *CH,* IV, XXIX (p. 99).

50. *AP* III, chap. III, 147 (p. 315 Conguy); *AG* II, app., 40 (p. 768 Jacobs); *AG* III (p. 896 n. 40); compare also *CCAG* 8³ (p. 73, frag. 237 Boudreaux).

51. Compare *AG* IX, 491 (pp. 302–303 Beckby); *AG* III, 491 (pp. 272–273 Paton). This monostich, however, is also ascribed to Pseudo-Manethon and Empedocles (*CH* IV, p. 99, app. crit.).

52. The appearance in the poem of Aion, a god prominent since the time of Iamblicus, proves that it was composed in the late Hellenic period. On the god Aion in Neoplatonism see John F. Finamore, *Iamblichus and the Theory of the Vehicle of the Soul* (Chico, Calif., 1985), pp. 133–135; Bowersock, *Hellenism in Late Antiquity,* pp. 23–27, 51, 57.

53. In two Parisian codexes the poem is connected with the name Theon of Alexandria. Compare *CCAG* 8³ (p. 74, frags. 261 and 261v Boudreaux); *AP* III, 3, 146 (pp. 314–315 Conguy); *AG* II, app., 39 (p. 768 Jacobs); *AG* III (p. 895 and n. 39).

54. On the Orphic views about man's origin, destiny, and soul, see L. J. Alderink, *Creation and Salvation in Ancient Orphism* (Ann Arbor, 1981), pp. 63, 76–77. On Orphism and Orpheus himself (he was revived in Neoplatonism and in various currents of late Hellenism) see, among others, Bowersock, *Hellenism in Late Antiquity,* pp. 31, 36, 41, 47.

55. *AG,* VII, 292 (p. 174 Beckby); *AG* IX, 41 (p. 34 Beckby).

56. *AG,* IX, 175 (p. 110 Beckby).

57. *AG,* IX, 202 (p. 124 Beckby).

58. Compare *CCAG,* 4 (p. 125, frag. 172, and p. 154, frag. 433v Heeg); 5³ (p. 141, frag. 33 Heeg); 6 (pp. 79–80, frag. 143v Heeg).

59. G. Fowden, *The Egyptian Hermes* (Cambridge, 1986), pp. 177–186; Haas, pp. 221–222.

60. See J. A. Fabricius, *Bibliotheca Graeca,* IV, 140–144; W. Gundel and H. G. Gundel, *Astrologumena. Die astrologische Literatur in der Antike und ihre Geschichte* (Wiesbaden, 1966), pp. 236–239.

61. Gundel and Gundel, *Astrologumena,* pp. 239–241.

62. Ibid., pp. 241–242.

63. *De insomniis* 1. On the philosophical concepts in this work see Kissling in *American Journal of Philology* 43 (1922):318–330; Bregman, pp. 145–154; also see Chapter II, note 90. We learn from Damascius (*Epit. Phot.* 12, pp. 12–13 Zintzen) that the philosopher Isidore was endowed with the gift of divination through dreams, a characteristic skill of the Alexandrians.

64. On this list of "holy men" see Fowden in *Classical Philology* 80 (1985):284.

65. On the influence of Hermeticism on Synesius see Chapter II, note 92.

66. M. Clagett considers the term *hydrometer* more adequate for this kind of equipment (*The Science of Mechanics in the Middle Ages,* Madison, 1959, p. 91). Clagett observes that according to an Arabian source a similiar hydrometer is said to have been constructed by Pappus, Theon's senior colleague.

67. Lacombrade (1951), pp. 42–43. Cameron is closest to the truth (1993), p. 87 and n. 196.

68. *CCAG* 82 (p. 113 Ruelle); Gundel and Gundel, *Astrologumena,* p. 243. *CCAG* 82 (p. 141.17–19 Ruelle) describes the nature of the hydromancer's work: "Hydromancis sunt qui in aqua inspectione umbras daemonum evocant et imagines vel ludificationes ibi videre et ab aliis aliqua audire se perhibent."

69. Cf. Lacombrade (1951), pp. 65–68; Cameron (1993), pp. 53–54.

70. Rougé (1990), p. 487, observes that Theophilus did not particularly differ from his predecessors (or successors) in the persecution of paganism and that he acted in accordance with the existing law.

71. For a critical examination of sources on the destruction of the Serapis cult see J. Schwarz, "La fin du Sérapéum d'Alexandrie," *American Studies in Papyrology* 1 (1966):97–111. G. Fowden, "Bishops and Temples in the Eastern Roman Empire, A.D. 320–434," *Journal of Theological Studies*, n.s. 29.1 (1978):69–70.

72. See Schwarz, "La fin du Sérapéum," p. 110; Chuvin, pp. 65–66, accepts 391. Bowersock, too, calls attention to the findings connected with the date 392; *Hellenism in Late Antiquity*, p. 59 and n. 17.

73. C.Th. XVI.10, 11; Schwarz, "La fin du Sérapéum," p. 107.

74. For a characterization of the pagan population in the fourth and fifth centuries in Alexandria see Haas, pp. 196–284.

75. Ibid., pp. 245–246; Chuvin, p. 67.

76. A. Cameron, *Claudian Poetry and Propaganda at the Court of Honorius* (Oxford, 1970), pp. 28–29, 199–208.

77. *PRLE*, I, 658; Cameron in *Journal of Roman Studies* 55 (1965):26–27; Chuvin, pp. 66–67.

78. See Chuvin, chaps. 5 and 6. Antoninus' prophecy proclaimed that "after his death the temple would cease to be, and even the great and holy temples of Serapis would pass into formless darkness and be transformed, and that a fabulous and unseemly gloom would hold sway over the fairest things on earth" (*VS* VI.9.17); Haas, p. 253; Penella, p. 59 n. 46.

79. Rufinus, *HE* XI.22–30; Sozomenos, *HE* VII.15; Dam. frags. pp. 69–75 Zintzen.

80. Dam., *Epit. Phot.* 48 (p. 70 Zintzen) = frag. 92 (pp. 69–71).

81. Dam. frag. 91 (p. 69 Zintzen).

82. Dam. frag. 97 (p. 73 Zintzen).

83. *HE* V.16.

84. Sozomenos, *HE* VII.15.

85. A biography of Antoninus is found in Eunapius, *VS* VI.9.15–17 and VI.10.5–11, 12. On the chronology of Antoninus' life see Penella, p. 54. On the destruction of the temple in Canopus with the participation of monks, see G. J. Bartelink, "Les rapports entre le monachisme égyptien et l'épiscopat d'Alexandrie," in *Alexandrina: Mélanges offerts à Claude Mondésert* (Paris, 1987), p. 374.

86. *VS* VI.10.7. Penella (pp. 59, 142) places Antoninus among typical philosophers pursuing the "Iamblichan" kind of philosophizing.

87. A. Fliche and V. Martin, *Histoire de l'église depuis les origines jusqu'à nos jours,* I (Paris, 1936), pp. 134ff.; H. W. G. Liebeschuetz, "The Fall of John Chrysostom," *Nottingham Medieval Studies* 30 (1985):7; C. W. Griggs, *Early Egyptian Christianity: From Its Origins to 451 C.E.* (Leiden, New York, Copenhagen, Cologne, 1990), pp. 185f.

88. J. Kopallik was the first to introduce Cyril in a positive light, stressing his theological accomplishments: *Cyrillus von Alexandrien: Eine Biographie nach den Quellen gearbeitet* (Mainz, 1881). At present see, among others, *Kyrilliana: Specilegia edita Sancti Cyrilli Alexandrini XV recurrente saeculo* (Cairo, 1947); A. Kerrigan, *St. Cyril of Alexandria: Interpreter of the Old Testament* (Rome, 1952); E. Gebremedhin, *Life-Giving Blessing: An Inquiry into the Eucharistic Doctrine of Cyril of Alexandria* (Uppsala, 1977); J. Liébaert, *La doctrine chritologique de Saint Cyrille d'Alexandrie avant la querelle Nestorienne* (Lille, 1951); P. Imhof and B. Lorenz, *Maria Theotokos bei Cyrill von Alexandrien. Zur Theotokos Tradition und ihrer Relevanz* (Munich, 1981); *Cyril of Alexandria: Select Letters,* ed. L. R. Wickham (Oxford, 1983). The best characterization of Cyril comes from W. H. C. Frend, *The Rise of Monophysite Movement Chapters in the History of the Church in the Fifth and Sixth Centuries* (Cambridge, 1972), p. 16: "He was a master-theologian whose deep perception of the mystery of the incarnation has influenced Greek theology from that day to this, and he could formulate his ideas in such a way as to make them appear acceptable in the West also. Against this he was utterly unscrupulous, overbearing, turbulent and greedy for power, ready to use the mob and the monks to do his bidding against his opponents such as the Alexandrian Jews and the pagans."

89. Socrates, *HE* VII.7; *PRLE,* II, 3 (Abundantius 1).

90. Rougé (1990), p. 486. This view contradicts the commonly held opinion that Abundantius represented the interests of Theodosius II, who wanted to establish his own candidate in the Alexandrian patriarchate.

91. Socrates, *HE* VII.7.

92. Ibid.; Rougé (1990), pp. 487–488.

93. *HE* VII.13.

94. A. C. Johnson, *Egypt and the Roman Empire* (Ann Arbor, 1951), p. 145.

95. On the relations between the Jewish community and the Chris-

tians in Alexandria in late antiquity see R. J. Wilken, *Judaism and the Early Christian Mind: A Study of Cyril of Alexandria's Exegesis and Theology* (New Haven, 1971), especially pp. 54ff.; W. D. Barry, "Faces of the Crowd: Popular Society and Politics of Roman Alexandria, 30 B.C.–A.D. 215" (Ph.D. diss., University of Michigan, 1988), pp. 104–135; Haas, pp. 124–195; Rougé (1990), pp. 489–490.

96. On the conduct of the monks of Nitria and Scetis during that time see P. D. Scott-Moncrieff, *Paganism and Christianity in Egypt* (Cambridge, 1913), pp. 198–219; H. G. Evelyn-White, ed., *The Monasteries of the Wadi'n Natrû*, vol. 2: *The History of the Monasteries of Nitria and of Scetis* (New York, 1932), pp. 125–149; Hardy, *Christian Egypt,* pp. 87ff.; Frend, *The Rise of Monophysite Movement Chapters,* pp. 16, 73, 155, 263, 270, 326; P. Rousseau, *Ascetics, Authority and the Church in the Age of Jerome and Cassian* (Oxford, 1978), pp. 9–11; Lizzi in *Atti dell'Istituto Veneto di scienze, lettere ed arti* 141 (1982–83):127–145.

97. As mentioned earlier, Orestes was baptized by Bishop Atticus. Rougé (1990), pp. 492–493, believes that Orestes' admission that he had been baptized by Atticus infuriated the monks even more because Atticus was John Chrysostom's ally, Theophilus' antagonist. On Atticus see Fliche and Martin, *Histoire de l'église,* IV (Paris, 1945), pp. 150ff.

98. *HE* VII.15.

99. Dam. frag. 102 (p. 79.12–13 Zintzen).

100. Haas, p. 244.

101. We do not know the date of Orestes' assumption of office in Egypt or of the beginning of the anti-Jewish riots. But the year 414 is generally accepted as the date of the conflict (Wilken, *Judaism and the Early Christian Mind,* p. 56). On the prerogatives of the prefect of Egypt see H. Last, "The Praefectus Aegypti and His Powers," *Journal of Egyptian Archaeology* 40 (1954):68–73.

102. *HE* VII.13; see also Haas, p. 259.

103. Haas, p. 253.

104. Cyril probably suspected that young priests were attending Hypatia's lectures. Rougé (1990), p. 496, assumes that in his youth Cyril himself attended them.

105. Cameron (1993), chaps. III, 1; V; VI, 3, argues that Aurelian was not Synesius' close acquaintance, that he did not belong to the circle of his friends in Constantinople.

106. Dam. frag. 102 (p. 79.13–14 Zintzen).

107. Rougé (1990), pp. 499–500, is in error in thinking that Hypatia exerted influence on the Alexandrian masses through the upper-class people with whom she maintained spiritual and political contact.

108. *Chron.* 84–87 (pp. 100–102 Charles). For the criminal law on magic, witchcraft, sorcerers, and wizards see C.Th. 9, 16.1–9, 10. Compare F. H. Cramer, *Astrology in Roman Law and Politics* (Philadelphia, 1954), especially pp. 276–283; Chuvin, pp. 30–31, 39–40.

109. *Suda,* s.v. Hypatia 4 (644.7–8 Adler). It is generally held that in those times mathematics was grouped with astrology and magic as *ars mathematica;* compare Haas, pp. 221–222, 254. As early as 1879, Ligier (pp. 78ff.) maintained that Hypatia's scholarly interest in mathematics was used to accuse her of magic; the accusation became the reason for her death.

110. Dam. frag. 102 (p. 81.1 Zintzen).

111. Hoche, p. 462, claims (like Gibbon before) that they were seashells, for Caesarion was located close to the shore, near the Great Port (Haas, pp. 215–216).

112. It is an unknown location; see Kopallik, *Cyrillus von Alexandrien,* p. 24 n. 1; Hoche, n. 106.

113. *Chronogr.,* p. 359 Bonn.

114. *Suda,* s.v. Hypatia 4 (644.5–6 Adler).

115. Dam. frag. 102 (p. 81.7–10 Zintzen).

116. K. G. Holum, *Theodosian Empresses: Women and Imperial Dominion in Late Antiquity* (Berkeley, 1982), pp. 98–100. As early as 1886, Meyer (pp. 20–22) assumed that Hypatia fell victim to antipagan edicts of the Catholic state, issued until 415. On the anti-Jewish laws see Rougé (1990), p. 489 n. 24.

117. Cameron (1993), chap. III, 1.

118. Compare J. Vogt, *Das unverletzliche Gut: Synesios an Hypatia, Festschrift für Konstantinos J. Merentis* (Athens, 1972), pp. 431–437.

119. Following Meyer, pp. 29–32, some scholars have maintained that Synesius' quarrel with Cyril was the reason for Hypatia's death— that she fell victim as a third party to the conflict between Cyril and Orestes or between Cyril and Synesius, as a means of restraining their activity against Cyril. Meyer contends that Cyril had old accounts to

settle with Synesius. Some scholars suppose that *Ep.* 12 was not sent to Cyril the future archbishop.

120. C.Th. 16.2, 42. Le Nain de Tillemont was the first to discuss the parabolans' connection with Hypatia's death. See also A. Philipsborn, "La compagnie d'ambulanciers, Parabolani d'Alexandrie," *Byzantion* 20 (1950):185–190; W. Schubert, "Parabalani," *Journal of Egyptian Archaeology* 40 (1954):97, 101. In the context of Hypatia's death J. Rougé, "Les débuts de l'épiscopat de Cyrille d'Alexandrie et le code Théodosien," in *Alexandrina* (Paris, 1987), pp. 341–349.

121. Rougé, "Les débuts," pp. 346–348.

122. C.Th. 16.2, 43; Rougé, "Les débuts," p. 346; Rougé (1990), p. 501.

123. Compare J. Marlowe, *The Golden Age of Alexandria: From Its Foundation by Alexander the Great in 331 B.C. to Its Capture by the Arabs in 642 A.D.* (London, 1971), pp. 281, 288, 293–294; Hardy, *Christian Egypt,* p. 105; Holum, *Theodosian Empresses,* pp. 99–100, 166; Rougé, "Les débuts," p. 345.

124. E.g., Cameron (1993), p. 44.

125. *HE* VII.14.

126. (1993), p. 494.

127. As mentioned earlier, Philostorgius imputes the crime to orthodox Christians, to some group connected with the Alexandrian church and Cyril.

128. F. Schaefer, "St. Cyril of Alexandria and the Murder of Hypatia," *Catholic University Bulletin* 8.4 (1902):441–453.

129. Rougé (1991), p. 500.

130. *Suda,* s.v. Hypatia 4 (644.9–11 Adler).

131. *HE* VII.13.

132. Haas, p. 52 n. 58; more on the events connected with the murder of bishop George (pp. 230–240); Frend, *The Rise of Monophysite Movement Chapters,* pp. 142, 154–155 (Proterius).

133. On the Alexandrian people in the early empire see Barry, "Faces of the Crowd"; for the late empire see Haas, pp. 8, 74, and chap. 5 passim.

134. Dam. frag. 102 (p. 81.7 Zintzen).

135. Dam. frag. 276 (p. 219 Zintzen); the Alexandrians attended

the philosopher Isidore's lectures and heeded him "despite the well-founded dread which hung over him." Isidore's friend and the heir of his estate seldom left his house to appear in the streets (frag. 34, p. 33 Zintzen). Thus Hypatia's successors in the Alexandrian "school" distanced themselves from politics, confining themselves to private teaching of philosophy in their own homes. These circumstances reflected the general weakening of the Alexandrian intellectual circles.

Conclusion

1. As early as 1901, Crawford (pp. 398–399) asserted that Hypatia's death was related to the turmoil in Alexandria: "The cause of her death was much more political than religious. Alexandria was suffering from the discord between the heads of Church and State. The Christian rabble imagined that her influence embittered the strife, and thought that, if she were out of the way, a reconciliation might be effected. Accordingly they murdered her, not as an enemy to the Faith, but as a fancied hindrance to their temporal comforts." Many years later Rist, p. 224, expressed a similar view: "It seems that it was to this public activity and to her public position rather than to her purely philosophical or even astronomical interests that she owed her death."

2. Rougé (1990), pp. 501–503. Haas, p. 254, nevertheless contends that Hypatia's death inevitably constituted a phase in the conflict between the Christians and the pagan community.

3. See G. Fowden, *The Egyptian Hermes: A Historical Approach to the Late Pagan Mind* (Cambridge, 1986), p. 180. There seems to be no ground for Fowden's linking (p. 182) of Hypatia's death with the struggle of the church against Hermeticism at that time. Fowden himself points out that Cyril began his contention with pagan religious thought when writing his refutation of Julian the Apostate (pp. 181–183).

4. See T. Kobusch, *Studien zur Philosophie des Hierokles von Alexandrien. Untersuchungen zum christlichen Neuplatonismus* (Munich, 1976); Hadot, *Le problème du Néoplatonisme Alexandrin;* Aujoulat, *Le Néoplatonisme Alexandrin.*

5. For data on these philosophers see *PRLE,* II and III; *The Cambridge History of Later Greek and Early Medieval Philosophy,* III, ed. A. H. Armstrong (Cambridge, 1967), pp. 314–322; Wallis, *Neoplatonism,*

pp. 138–146; R. Sorabji in Philoponus, *Against Aristotle on the Eternity of the World,* trans. C. Wildberg (Ithaca, 1987), pp. 3–12.

6. Karren, "Near Eastern Culture and Hellenic Paideia," pp. xvi–xvii, rightly observes: "No other religious figures are more representative of paganism in the fifth century A.D. than the Alexandrian Neoplatonists." The situation of the pagans in the fifth and sixth centuries in Egypt and Alexandria is discussed by E. Wipszycka, "Problemy chrystianizacji Egiptu w. IV–VII. Aspekty społeczne i narodowościowe" (Problems in the Christianization of Egypt in the fourth–seventh centuries), in *Świat antyczny, Stosunki społeczne, ideologia i polityka, religia* (The world of antiquity: Social relations, ideology and politics, religion) (Warsaw, 1988), pp. 288–325.

7. On these philosophers see J. Maspero, "Horapollon et la fin du paganisme égyptien," *BIFAO* 11 (1914):163–165; R. Rémondon, "L'Egypte et la suprème résistance au christianisme," *BIFAO* 51 (1952):63–78; Fowden in *JHS* 102 (1982):46–48; Haas, pp. 223–227; Chuvin, pp. 106–111.

8. Their place in late Hellenic paganism and culture is best defined by Bowersock, *Hellenism in Late Antiquity,* pp. 60–61.

Sources

1. On eminent women in antiquity see Aegidius Menagius, *Historia mulierum philosopharum* (Amsterdam, 1692); J. C. Wolf, *Mulierum graecarum, quae oratione prosa usae sunt, fragments et elogia* (London, 1739); see also the survey in S. Wolf, *Hypatie die Philosophin von Alexandrien* (Vienna, 1879), pp. 7–11. Recent studies include M. Alic, *Hypatia's Heritage: A History of Women in Science from Antiquity through the Nineteenth Century* (Boston, 1986); K. Wider, "Women Philosophers in the Ancient Greek World," *Hypatia* 1.1 (1986):21–63; M. E. Waithe, ed., *A History of Women Philosophers,* vol. 1: *Ancient Women Philosophers, 600 B.C.–500 A.D.* (Dordrecht, Boston, Lancaster, 1987); J. McIntosh Snyder, *The Woman and the Lyre: Women Writers in Classical Greece and Rome* (Carbondale, 1989), pp. 113–121 on Hypatia.

2. *PRLE,* I, 202 (Chiona) and 338 (Gemina 1 and Gemina 2). These women Neoplatonists are discussed in Fowden (1979), pp. 100ff.; also Penella, p. 61.

3. *PRLE,* I, 57.

4. *PRLE,* I, 542.

5. Fowden (1979), p. 103; *PRLE,* I, 101.

6. *VS* VI.6–9.2 (pp. 28ff. Giangrande).

7. Penella, pp. 58–62. On Sosipatra also see *PRLE,* II, 849; G. Giangrande, "La profezia di Sosipatra in Eunapio," *Studi classici e orientali* 5 (1955):111–116; Fowden (1979), pp. 103–107; Fowden in *JHS* 102 (1982):37, 39, 55.

8. *PRLE,* II, 159 (Asclepigeneia 1); also Marinus, *Vita Procli* 28 and 29 (p. 84 Masullo).

9. H. Druon, *Etudes sur la vie et les oeuvres de Synésios, évêque de Ptolémais* (Paris, 1859), p. 10.

10. *PRLE,* II, 799; Marinus, *Vita Procli* 9 (p. 66 Masullo); on the philosopher Proclus see *PRLE,* II, 915–919.

11. *PRLE,* II, 10–11; *Suda,* s.v. Haidesia 2 (161.8–162.21 Adler) = Dam. frags. 105–109 (pp. 124–127 Zintzen); *Epit. Phot.* 76 (p. 106 Zintzen).

12. *PRLE,* II, 1051.

13. *PRLE,* II, 547–548.

14. *PRLE,* II, 71–72 (Ammonius 6); *PRLE,* II, 532 (Heliodorus 6).

15. De Lacy O'Leary, *The Saints of Egypt* (London and New York, 1937; reprint, Amsterdam, 1974), p. 261.

16. Wolf, *Mulierum graecarum* (1739), pp. 343–345; F. G. Holweck, *A Bibliographical Dictionary of the Saints* (St. Louis and London, 1924), p. 335.

17. See *Oxford Dictionary of Byzantium,* s.v. Mary of Egypt (New York, 1991).

18. *Leges novellae* Marc. 5, in P. R. Coleman-Norton, *Roman State and Christian Church: A Collection of Legal Documents to A.D. 535,* III (London, 1966), 488, pp. 849–852.

19. On St. Catherine, honored in both the East and the West, see Wolf, "Catherina patrona philosophorum," in *Mulierum graecarum,* pp. 305–311; G. B. Bronzini, "La leggenda di Sa Caterina d'Alessandria. Passioni greche e latine," *Atti della Accademia Nazionale dei Linzei,* 357, ser. 8, Memorie, Classe di scienze morali, storiche e filologiche, IX (Roma, 1960), pp. 255–413; also *Oxford Dictionary of Byzantium,* s.v.

20. Among others see A. B. Jameson, *Sacred and Legendary Art* (New

York, 1905), p. 475; Asmus in *Studien zur vergleichenden Literaturgeschichte* 7 (1907):18; *Lexicon für Theologie und Kirche,* VI, col. 60; H. Delehaye, "Les martyrs d'Egypte," *Analecta Bollandiana,* 40 (1922). At the beginning of the twentieth century the view was so widespread that it was even shared by J. McCabe, who wrote: "Perhaps we may see some reparation in the fact that a part of Hypatia's glory has crept into the canon of the Church, and is honored each year in the person of St. Catherine"; *The Critic* 43 (1903):272.

21. See B. A. Myrsilides in *Annuaire scientifique de la Faculté de philosophie de l'Université d'Athènes,* IIième Periode, 24 (1973–74): 418–420.

INDEX

Fabricius, Johann Albert, 24
Ferretti, André *(Renaissance en Paganie)*, 15, 102
Fielding, Henry *(A Journey from This World to the Next)*, 4
Fowden, G., 76

Gaius, 37
Garzya, A., 36, 37, 42, 43
George (bishop of Alexandria), 99
Gessius, 81
Gibbon, Edward *(Decline and Fall of the Roman Empire)*, 3–4, 19–20, 24
Gnosticism, 70
Gratian, 68
Greeks, 1, 2, 5, 7, 11, 41, 63, 69, 71, 83, 102

Haas, J. C., 76
Heliodorus, 40
Helladius, 80, 82
Hellenes, 13, 105
Hellenism, 3, 5–6, 11, 25, 30, 61, 62, 63, 65, 70, 74, 76, 83, 90
Hephaistion of Thebes, 77, 78
Heraclian, 10
Heraiskos, 106
Herculianus, and Synesius, 29–32, 32, 34, 35, 39, 42, 44, 47, 48, 52–53, 58, 59, 60, 89
Hermeias, 56
Hermes (Thoth), 63, 82
Hermes Trismegistus, 74, 75, 77, 78
Hermeticism, 63, 70, 76, 77, 102
Herodes, 38
Herodian, 37
Hesychius, 24, 35, 36, 44, 59, 67, 68, 69, 89; on Hypatia, 70, 71, 72, 91, 102; on Hypatia's murder, 93, 97, 98, 99
Hierax, 85, 90, 91
Hierocles, 105

Hoche, R., 25
Hölderlin, Friedrich, 5
Homer, 3, 9, 30
Honorius, 93
Horapollon the Older, 106
Horapollon the Younger, 106
Hypatia: A Journal of Feminist Philosophy, 16
Hypatia: Feminist Studies, 16

Iamblichus, 48, 62, 63, 80
Isidore (philosopher), 16, 24, 55, 63, 70
Isidore, Prince, 12
Isidore of Pelusium, 42, 43–44
Ision, 34–35
Isis, temple of, 104

Jacobacci, R., 25
Jews, 7, 8, 10, 85–86, 87, 88, 90, 91, 92, 94, 96, 104
John of Nikiu, 38–39, 44, 45, 64, 88–89, 90, 91, 92, 93, 97
John Philoponus, 105
Jone, 13, 14
Julian the Apostate, 7, 99, 104

Kinaron, 93
Kingsley, Charles *(Hypatia or the New Foes with an Old Face)*, 8–11, 15, 16, 22, 60, 68, 101
Knorr, W. R., 72

Lacombrade, C., 42, 43, 64, 78
Leconte de Lisle, Charles: *Hypatie*, 4–5, 8, 11, 101; "Hypatie et Cyrille," 5–7, 22
Leon the Philosopher, 76
Lewis, Thomas, 2
Libanius, 48, 63
Libya, 33, 34, 35, 36, 46, 66
Ligier, Hermann, 25
Luck, G., 23
Lumpkin, B., 25

Index ⁓ *157*

REVEALING ANTIQUITY

G. W. Bowersock, General Editor